NINJA FOODI
Cookbook 2023

ALMOST 200 SIMPLE, QUICK AND DELICIOUS
RECIPES TO IMPRESS YOUR FAMILY AND
FRIENDS. GRILL, PRESSURE COOK, AIR FRY,
CRISP AND BAKE WITH MANY DIFFERENT
NINJA MODELS!

Janet McKenzie

Table of Contents

CHAPTER 5
Easy Breakfasts

CHAPTER 6
Breakfasts

CHAPTER 7
Easy Vegetarian and Vegan Recipes 73

CHAPTER 8
Easy Chicken And Poultry Recipes 105

CHAPTER 9
Chicken And Poultry Recipes 133

CHAPTER 10

CHAPTER 14
Staples

CHAPTER 15
Desserts 271

CONCLUSION 291

INTRODUCTION

Imagine being able to sauté vegetables, steam rice, and cook the perfect steak in just one pot. That's right. You can prepare a meal that has all your daily nutritional requirements using only one appliance. Even better? You can make desserts like a cobbler and fla   in the very same unit.

The Ninja Foodi is not just for cooking food for adults. If you have a little one at home, you can use the Foodi to make healthy and delicious baby food, so you know exactly what you're feeding your child.

If you haven't heard about the Ninja Foodi, you should start reading this book, because not only will it offe   some of the most sumptuous recipes that you can ever stumble into, but it will also offe   you useful information that will help you understand the function of this new cooking appliance. So, if you are a Newbie in the use of Ninja Foodies, don't get frustrated, because, in this book, you will just find everything you need and enough information that will help you understand this cooking appliance better.

It is a single machine that can do the work of four machines. It can do everything that is done by an Instant Pot. It can even do much more than that. Also, the Ninja Foodi costs you less than the amount you have to pay for buying all other machines individually.

Sometimes the ease you feel at things is due to how friendly they behave towards you. It means that the more comfortable it is to use, the more you enjoy using it. Ninja Foodi is very easy to use, and you don't need to put in a lot of effor into understand how it *works*. It's easy to learn its usage and does not bother you much. There is a digital display given in Ninja Foodi whereas there is no such kind of technologically developed approach in an Instant Pot.

As the pressure keeps rising within Ninja Foodi, it continuously becomes visible at the digital display. Ninja Foodi is reliable because everything is visible on the digital display while in the case of Instant Pot it is not like that. It's all about how accurately you can guess.

Apart from other aspects comes the cleaning of Ninja Foodi. It's easy to clean Ninja Foodi and clear it from the food particles and oily content of your food. One who uses it can quickly get the trick of its efficie cleaning.

Note: this book is mainly based on recipes for the Ninja Foodi Pressure Cooker. Many of these recipes are also achievable with other Ninja models (depending on the specific cooking functions included in the model). Recipes that can only be made with the Ninja Foodi Grill are identified at the top by a "grill" icon.

Recipes suited mainly for "Pressure Cooker" but also achievable with other Ninja models:

Recipes suited for "Grill" model ONLY:

If you will like this recipes cookbook please leave a review!

CHAPTER 1

What Ninja Foodi Is and How It Works

Understanding the Ninja Foodi Multicooker

The Ninja Foodi Multicooker is a tabletop multi-function appliance that can grill, the air fry, bake, roast, sauté, pressure cook, broil and even dehydrate depending on the specific model. The Ninja Foodi Pressure Cooker (as an example) is a pressure cooler ,air fryer, convection oven, slow cooker, oven toaster, and dehydrator all rolled into one.

As you've probably guessed, the Ninja Foodi is not your average kitchen appliance because getting one for your home is like getting your own chef. The Ninja Foodi was developed through the collaboration of the Ninja engineers and a group of chefs who tested the unit at every stage of the product development. The result? Even those who have no prior cooking experience can make flavor-packe meals at home that the whole family will enjoy.

The Ninja Foodi is the first to combine a pressure cooker and another very popular kitchen appliance today: the air fryer. If you look around the market, there is no shortage of kitchen gadgets that combine the slow cooker and pressure-cooking functions. That's all well and good, but what if you want something fried and crispy? You'll have to take out either your frying pan or deep fryer to achieve the right crunch and color. This means you can make roast chicken that is juicy and tender within and beautiful bronzed and crisp outside.

The Benefits of Using an Electric Cooker

Whether it is a trend or the general convenience of it, more people are appreciating smaller and more portable indoor cookers due to several benefits from owning one.

Compact

Electric grills are small enough to fit most kitchen counters and tables. It is also portable enough to be easily transported or moved around.

Smokeless

This is probably one of the best things about indoor electric cooker. People who do not have any access to open areas can still enjoy grilling since it does not produce smoke like standard grillers.

Multi-function

Most indoor cookers come with various functionalities giving you more value for your money. It can also eliminate the need to purchase other appliances and save you essential kitchen space.

Easy to clean and operate

Indoor cookers are plug and play appliances making them user-friendly to a wider demographic. The cooking components are coated with a non-stick ceramic material that can be effortlessl taken apart and cleaned using a standard dishwasher.

Ninja Foodi Combines Pressure Cooker with Air Fryer

If you look around the market, there is no shortage of kitchen gadgets that combine the slow cooker and pressure cooking functions. That's all well and good, but what if you want something fried and crispy? You'll have to take out either your frying pan or deep fryer to achieve the right crunch and color.

It Works Automatically

Having a Ninja Foodi is like having a reliable kitchen assistant. For example, you forget that you were cooking something. When the cooking time is over, the Foodi automatically switches to the Keep Warm mode so your food will be the perfect temperature for when you're ready to eat.

It Helps You Plan Meals Ahead of Time

When you know you only need one kitchen appliance to prepare everything from entree to dessert, meal planning becomes easy. You can create a weekly schedule of meals that use the same ingredients to cut back on your prep time as well as costs.

It is Healthy for Human Beings

Fried foods are chock-full of calories and fats, which is why most healthy diets recommend that you cut back on your intake of foods cooked in fat if you want to lose weight.

Eating less fried foods is also ideal if you want to have good health in general because frying food can produce compounds like acrylamide, which is classified as a "possible carcinogen," according to the International Agency for Research on Cancer.

It is Quick and Timesaving

Who wouldn't eat delicious food every day? But even if you have some free time, you wouldn't want to spend it slaving away in the kitchen. If you've never had a complete and flavorfu meal of juicy chicken thighs, fragrant Basmati rice, and tender-crisp broccoli and carrots, plus a mouthwatering peach cherry crumble in under one hour, the Foodi can make it possible.

It Uses Less Oil

Ever tried cooking French fries or onion rings the old-fashioned way? Then, you know just how much oil it takes for the food to crisp up perfectly. With the Ninja Foodi, you don't even have to use oil at all. If you want to boost the crunch, a spritz of fat is all you need.

The other benefit of using less oil when cooking is that you don't have to deal with the splatters, which typically happens no matter how much you dry the food before cooking.

It Saves Energy

If you use your oven in the summer, you know just how hot the kitchen can get. Because it gets very hot, you'll need to up the air-conditioning just so you won't collapse from heat exhaustion.

Cooking with the Ninja Foodi is much more comfortable and energy saving at the same time. The appliance isn't only more efficie   than an oven, it won't turn your house into a sauna.

It Makes Dishes Tender Inside and Crispy Outside

The air frying function, which uses superheated steam to add another layer of flavo and moisture to the dish, allows you to have chicken with crisp and golden-brown skin without getting anywhere near a deep-fryer. That's why the Ninja Foodi is one-of-a-kind. You get the benefits of pressure cooking and air frying in one nifty appliance. You'll be looking forward to eating home cooked meals every day and you won't feel the need to eat out ever again!

It can Cook Frozen Ingredients

Having a Ninja Foodi means you won't have to worry about thawing ingredients before cooking them. In 30 minutes, you can enjoy perfectly cooked steak or crispy chicken wings.

How? By using the pressure-cooking function to defrost and tenderize the ingredients, then air-frying them afterward. This means you no longer have to order takeout even if you got home a little late from work.

The Food Will be Nutritious and Delicious

Cooking with the Ninja Foodi lets you create not just delicious and flavorfu meals but also nutritional foods as well. This is particularly true with vegetables that are pressure-cooked or steamed.

Grill marks

Like traditional outdoor grills, indoor grills can also give meat and other foods those appetizing grill marks. Although, the Ninja Foodi's grill marks are curved, unlike the typical straight markings you get from regular outdoor grills.

Browns and crisps food

Indoor grills like the Ninja Foodi use the circulating hot air to cook the food thoroughly. This creates delectable flavor through a browning process called the Maillard reaction. Similar to convection ovens and toasters, the Ninja Foodi is excellent at making food crunchy when you need it to be.

Capable of cooking at high temperatures

A wide range of temperature settings let you cook a variety of foods from char-grilled vegetables to restaurant-level steaks. Unlike other table top cookers, the Ninja Foodi will let you cook frozen foods without the need to defrost. It can also get as hot as 500° to 510° Fahrenheit / around 260° C.

Healthier Fried Food

For many people, fried food is the best comfort food. Whether it's fried chicken, French fries, or fried street food, everyone has probably at least one fried food included on their guilty pleasure list.

Having tried it yourself, you know that frying makes your food taste delicious and crispy. However, while the flavo of foods burst in your mouth, sometimes you just can't help but think about how many calories you get from eating greasy foods.

Well, that's right, we all know how it's done. You need oil to fry, oftentimes, you need lots of it. And from what we know, too much oil on food is bad news. But did you know that it is possible to have tasty and crunchy food without having to drench your meal in oil?

Air fryers have become some of the hottest kitchen appliances today that make frying easier without the guilt. This kitchen gadget was invented to replace your traditional oil fryer with air to make it a healthy alternative to frying with oil. This innovation has been gaining a footing in many countries in the west and thus far has been making a differenc in the way households prepare their food.

By definition, an air fryer is a kitchen appliance that cooks food by circulating hot air via a convection mechanism. The hot air is circulated at high speed around the food by a mechanical fan, cooking the food and making it crispy.

In America, the severe effect of obesity have been associated with the consumption of too much oily food. The use of air fryers has been gaining praise due to its promising offe as a beneficial solution to the long-existing problem of obesity as a result of eating oil-filled food. Its auspicious contribution in making a healthier lifestyle through healthy eating is what makes these types of gizmos very appealing, especially to those who are trying to lose weight and those who are aiming for healthier living.

The Structural Composition of the Ninja Foodi Cooker

Although the Ninja Foodi is a countertop cooker, it does come in a hefty size. But given its multi-purpose functionality and convenience over conventional single-purpose appliances, the size can easily be excused.

All cooking components are safe to use as it is manufactured without harmful chemicals such as PTFE, PFOA, and BPA.

The hood houses the heating element and convection fans that help sear meat and eliminate the need to fli food. All the accessories, included and optionals, for every Ninjia Foodie models are all coated with a non-stick ceramic finish

A grease collector at the back prevents any spillage and makes cleaning a breeze. The kebab skewers and roasting rack are all made of food-safe stainless steel as well.

The power cable is 10 feet / 3 meters long and is intended to keep the cooker close to an outlet and prevent people from tripping over lengthy cords.

How Does It Work?

The Ninja Foodi uses superheated steam to infuse moisture into the food using the pressure-cooking function. Then, with the powerful crisping lid, the machine releases rapid-hot air down and all around the food to create the crispy finis characteristic of fried foods without having to use a lot of oil.

Each Ninja Foodi comes with the Cook & Crisp basket, which allows you to cook a 5 lb. / 2.5 kg chicken, 2 lb. / 900g of chicken wings, or 3 lb. / 1.5 kg of French fries.

The default length of the Keep Warm mode is 12 hours, and you'll see the unit counting down. This way, you know how long the Ninja Foodi has been keeping your food warm at a temperature that is safe for consumption.

As an alternative, you can cook big batches of food during the weekend (or whenever you have free time, so you have your meals sorted throughout the week.

Another way to get a head start on your meal prep is to roast a whole chicken or make pulled pork out of boneless pork butt. Set these aside until you are ready to add them to salads, sandwiches, and other dishes like fried rice.

Of course, the pressure-cooking function is excellent for extracting flavo from the chicken, pork, or beef bones along with vegetable scraps and making a delicious stock to be used as a soup base for noodles or pasta.

CHAPTER 2

How To Properly Use The Ninja Foodi For Best Results

When you are cooking for the firs time with your Foodi, you must firs wash the detachable cooking parts with warm soapy water to remove any oil and debris. Let them air fry and place them back inside once you are ready to cook. An easy-to-follow instruction guide comes with each unit, so make sure to go over it before cooking.

For grilling

Plug your unit into an outlet and power on the grill.

Position your grill on a level and secure surface. Leave at least 6 inches of space around it, especially at the back where the air intake vent and air socket are located. Ensure that the splatter guard is installed whenever the grill is in use. This is a wire mesh that covers the heating element on the inside of the lid.

Use the grill grate over the cooking pot and choose the grill function. This has four default temperature settings of low at 400° F / 105° C, medium at 450° F / 230° C, high at 500° F / 260° C, and max at 510° F / 265° C.

Set the time needed to cook. You may check the grilling cheat sheet that comes with your unit to guide you with the time and temperature settings. It is best to check the food regularly depending on the doneness you prefer and to avoid overcooking.

Once the required settings are selected, press start and wait for the digital display to show 'add food'. The unit will start to preheat similar to an oven and will show the progress through the display. This step takes about 8 minutes.

If you need to check the food or fli it, the timer will pause and resume once the lid is closed.

The screen will show 'Done' once the timer and cooking have been completed. Power off the unit and unplug the device. Leave the hood open to let the unit cool faster.

For roasting

Remove the grill grates and use the cooking pot that comes with the unit. You may also purchase their roasting rack for this purpose.

Press the roast option and set the timer between 1 to 4 hours depending on the recipe requirements. The Foodi will preheat for 3 minutes regardless of the time you have set.

Once ready, place the meat directly on the roasting pot or rack. Check occasionally for doneness. A meat thermometer is another useful tool to get your meats perfectly cooked.

For baking

Remove the grates and use the cooking pot.

Choose the bake setting and set your preferred temperature and time. Preheating will take about 3 minutes.

Once done with preheating, you may put the ingredients directly on the cooking pot, or you may use your regular baking tray. An 8 inch / 20cm baking tray can fit inside as well as similar-sized oven-safe containers.

For air frying/air crisping

Put the crisper basket in and close the lid.

Press the "Air Crisp" or "Air Fry" option then the start button. The default temperature is set at 390° F / 200° C and will preheat at about 3 minutes. You can adjust the temperature and time by pressing the buttons beside these options.

If you do not need to preheat, just press the air crisp button a second time and the display will show you the 'add food' message.

Put the food inside and shake or turn every 10 minutes. Use oven mitts or tongs with silicone when doing this.

For dehydrating

Place the firs layer of food directly on the cooking pot.

Add the "Crisper" basket or the "Cook & Crisp" basket and add one more layer.

Choose the dehydrate setting and set the timer between 7 to 10 hours.

You may check the progress from time to time.

For cooking frozen foods

Choose the medium heat, which is 450° F / 230° C using the grill option. You may also use the air crisp option if you are cooking fries, vegetables, and other frozen foods.

Set the time needed for your recipe. Add a few minutes to compensate for the thawing.

Flip or shake after a few minutes to cook the food evenly.

CHAPTER 3

How To Clean And Maintain Your Ninja Foodi

Cleaning and Maintenance

Components are dishwasher-safe and are fabricated with a non-stick ceramic coating, to make clean-up and maintenance easier. Plus, the Ninja conveniently comes with a plastic cleaning brush with a scraper at the other end.

Cleaning Tips:

- Let the cooker cool down completely and ensure that it is unplugged from the power outlet before trying to clean the unit.

- Take out the removable parts and/or accessiories, and soak in soapy water for a few hours to let the debris soften and make cleaning easier. Wash only the removable parts.

- Gently brush off dirt and debris using the plastic brush that comes with your grill. Use the other end of the brush to dislodge food in hard to reach areas.

- Let the parts dry thoroughly.

- Clean the insides and exterior of the unit with a clean damp cloth.

Maintenance Tips:

- Always keep your unit clean, especially before putting in a new batch for cooking. You should clean the parts and the unit after each use.

- Never use cleaning instruments or chemicals that are too harsh and can damage the coating.

- Keep the electrical cords away from children and any traffic in your kitchen.

- Avoid getting the unit and electrical components wet and place it away from areas that constantly get soaked or damp.

- Always unplug the unit when not in use.

Troubleshooting

Smoke coming out of the Ninja

Although the Ninja Foodi is virtually smokeless as advertised, you may see some smoke from time to time for several reasons.

- One is the type of oil you use for cooking. Ideally, canola, grapeseed, and avocado oil should be used since they have a high smoke point. This means that they do not produce smoke or burn at high temperatures. Other oils with high smoke points include corn, almond, safflowe sesame, and sunflowe oils.

- Another reason is the accumulation of grease at the bottom of the pot. If you continuously cook foods that produce a lot of grease and oil, this will burn and create smoke. Empty and clean the pot before cooking the next batch.

The Ninja is showing 'Add Food'

This means that the unit has finishe preheating and that you can now put food inside the cooker.

The control panel is showing 'Shut Lid'

Try opening the lid and closing it securely until the message is gone.

The unit is unresponsive and only showing 'E' on the panel

Your unit is damaged, and you need to contact customer service.

CHAPTER 4

Ninja Foodi Pressure Cooker Basics: Main Functions and General Instructions

Function Buttons:

Pressure

The pressure cooker button is used to tenderize food quickly while locking in all the moisture and flavor

Steam

The steam function uses heated water vapor to cook delicate foods gently at a high temperature. This is ideal for perfectly cooking fish and vegetables.

Slow Cook

The slow cooker function cooks food at a lower temperature for longer lengths of time. This is great for dishes like pulled pork and fall-off-the-bon   pork/beef ribs.

Sear/Sauté

The searing/sautéing function transforms the Ninja Foodi into a stove top for sautéing vegetables like garlic and onions, simmering sauces, browning meats before stewing/braising for more flavor as well as a host of other uses.

Air Fry/Air Crisp

The air-frying function is great for making crisp foods like French fries, zucchini wedges, and onion rings without having to deep-fry them. This function is ideal for making golden-skinned roast chicken or roast pork belly with crackling.

Bake/Roast

The baking/roasting function transforms the Ninja Foodi into an oven so you can make baked treats, tender meats, and even pizza with a crisp cheesy top.

Broil

The broiling function allows you to caramelize or brown food. You can do this at the start of the cooking process to caramelize the sugar in meats and vegetables for a more flavorfu stew or broth.

Dehydrate (Only Available in Certain Models)

The dehydrating function lets you make dehydrated fruits, vegetables, and meats for healthy snacking as well as to increase the shelf life of these food items.

Operating Buttons:

Temp Arrows

The TEMP arrows allow you to adjust the cooking temperature and/or pressure level by pressing the up and down buttons accordingly.

Time arrows

The TIME arrows allow you to adjust the cooking time using the up and down buttons.

Start/Stop

To start cooking, press the "Start/Stop" button after selecting the temperature/ pressure and time. To stop the machine's cooking function, press the "Start/Stop" button again.

Keep Warm

This button automatically switches on after steaming, slow cooking, pressure cooking, or another cooking function is finished The "Keep Warm" mode will stay on for 12 hours. To turn off the mode, just press the "Keep Warm" button. The "Keep Warm" button keeps food warm at a food-safe temperature. In other words, it is not meant to be used to warm food from a cold/frozen state.

Power

This button shuts off the unit and stops all modes of cooking.

Standby Mode

The unit will enter "StandBy Mode" when there is no interaction with the control panel for 10 minutes.

Steps of Using Ninja Foodi

Before using your Ninja Foodi for the first time, make sure to do the following:

- Remove all the packaging material, tape, and promotional labels. Discard these using proper segregation protocols.

- Remove all the accessories from the package.

- Read the manual, paying special attention to instructions on how to operate the unit, usage warnings, as well as crucial safety tips to prevent damage and injury.

- Using hot, soapy water, wash the silicone ring, condensation collector, removable cooking pot, Reversible Rack, Cook & Crisp Basket, and pressure lid. Rinse and dry these accessories thoroughly. Check the pressure to make sure no debris is in the valves. IMPORTANT NOTE: Never place the pressure lid or the cooker base in the dishwasher.

- Place the silicone ring around the outer edge of the silicone ring rack under the lid. Make sure it is completely inserted and that it is lying fla under the silicone ring rack. Before each use, the silicone ring should be well seated in the silicone ring rack and the anti-clog cap must be mounted correctly on the pressure release valve.

- Install the condensation collector by sliding it into the slot found on the cooker base. To remove, slide it out.

Once you've done all the previous steps, you can begin using your Ninja Foodi.

To give you an idea of how easy it is to use the Ninja Foodi, take a look at the following are steps to making ginger rice with marinated chicken:

- Marinate about 2 lb. / 900gof chicken thighs in soy sauce, lime juice, garlic, minced ginger, green onions, and chilies (optional) for at least 30 minutes.

- Wash a cup of Basmati rice before placing it in the main cooking pot with 1 cup of water, chopped ginger, chopped green onions, a few drops of sesame oil, and some salt.

- Place the Reversible Rack in the cooking pot on top of the rice. Place the chicken (without the marinade) on the low rack.

- Place the pressure lid on the Ninja Foodi and turn to lock in place.

- Press the "Power" button, then press "Pressure". The default temperature is HI.

- Set the timer to 4 minutes. Then, press the "Start/Stop" button.

- When the pressure cooking is done, allow the Ninja Foodi to go into "Keep Warm" mode for 10 minutes.

- When the pressure valve is down, remove the pressure lid.

- Arrange green beans around the chicken and spritz a bit of oil on the surface of the meat and vegetables. Put the air crisping lid down.

- Press the "Air Fry" button and set the temperature to 400° F / 205° C for 15 minutes, to begin with. Check the doneness of the food mid-way and decide whether to adjust the length of cooking time or not.

CHAPTER 5

Easy Breakfasts

Simple Zucchini Egg Muffins

PREPARATION
5-10 min

COOKING
7 min

SERVING
4

INGREDIENTS

- 4 whole eggs
- 2 tablespoons almond flou
- 1 zucchini, grated
- 1 teaspoon butter
- ½ teaspoon salt

DIRECTIONS

1. Take a small-sized bowl and add almond flour salt, zucchini. Mix well

2. Take muffin molds and grease them gently, add the zucchini mix

3. Arrange your molds in Ninja Foodi and cook on "Air Fry" mode for 7 minutes at a temperature of 375° F / 190° C

4. Serve and enjoy the meal once complete!

Spinach Quiche

PREPARATION
10 min

COOKING
4 hours

SERVING
4

INGREDIENTS

- 10 ounces frozen chopped spinach, thawed and squeezed
- 4 ounces' feta cheese, shredded
- 2 cups unsweetened almond milk
- 4 organic eggs
- ¼ teaspoon red pepper flakes crushed
- Salt and ground black pepper, as required

DIRECTIONS

1. In the pot of Ninja Foodie, add all the ingredients and mix until well combined.
2. Close the Ninja Foodi with a crisping lid and select "Slow Cook".
3. Set on "Low" for 4 hours.
4. Press "Start/Stop" to begin cooking.
5. Cut into equal-sized wedges and serve hot.

Nuts & Seeds Granola

PREPARATION
15 min

COOKING
120 min

SERVING
12

INGREDIENTS

- 1/3 cup unsalted butter
- 1 teaspoon liquid stevia
- 1 teaspoon organic vanilla extract
- 1½ cups pumpkin seeds
- 1½ cups sunflowe seeds
- ½ cup raw pecans, chopped roughly
- ½ cup raw hazelnuts, chopped roughly
- ½ cup raw walnuts, chopped roughly
- ½ cup raw almonds, chopped roughly
- 1 teaspoon ground cinnamon

DIRECTIONS

1. Select the "Sauté/Sear" setting of Ninja Foodi and place the butter into the pot.
2. Press "Start/Stop" to begin cooking and heat for about 2-3 minutes.
3. Include the flui stevia and vanilla concentrate and mix to combine.
4. Immediately, press "Start/Stop" to stop cooking
5. Now, add the remaining ingredients and stir to combine.
6. Close the Ninja Foodi with a crisping lid and select "Slow Cook".
7. Set on "Low" for 2 hours, stirring after every 30 minutes.
8. Press "Start/Stop" to begin cooking.
9. Move the granola onto an enormous heating sheet and set aside to cool completely before serving.

Cinnamon French Toast

PREPARATION
10 min

COOKING
6 min

SERVING
2

INGREDIENTS

- 2 eggs
- ¼ cup whole milk
- 3 tablespoons sugar
- 2 teaspoons olive oil
- 1/8 teaspoon vanilla extract
- 1/8 teaspoon ground cinnamon
- 4 bread slices

DIRECTIONS

1. In a large bowl, mix all the ingredients except bread slices.
2. Coat the bread slices with egg mixture evenly.
3. Press the "Power Button" of Air Fry Oven and turn the dial to select the "Air Fry" mode.
4. Press the Time button and again turn the dial to set the cooking time to 6 minutes.
5. Now push the Temp button and rotate the dial to set the temperature at 390° F / 200° C.
6. Press the "Start/Pause" button to start.
7. When the unit beeps to show that it is preheated, open the lid and lightly grease the sheet pan.
8. Arrange the bread slices into "Air Fry Basket" and insert it in the oven.
9. Flip the bread slices once halfway through.
10. Serve warm.

Sweet Spiced Toast

PREPARATION
10 min

COOKING
4 min

SERVING
3

INGREDIENTS

- ¼ cup of sugar
- ½ teaspoon ground cinnamon
- 1/8 teaspoon ground cloves
- 1/8 teaspoon ground ginger
- ½ teaspoons vanilla extract
- ¼ cup salted butter softened
- 6 bread slices

DIRECTIONS

1. In a bowl, add the sugar, vanilla, cinnamon, pepper, and butter. Mix until smooth.
2. Spread the butter mixture evenly over each bread slice.
3. Press the "Power Button" of Air Fry Oven and turn the dial to select the "Air Fry" mode.
4. Press the Time button and again turn the dial to set the cooking time to 4 minutes.
5. Now push the Temp button and rotate the dial to set the temperature at 400° F / 205° C.
6. Press the "Start/Pause" button to start.
7. When the unit beeps to show that it is preheated, open the lid and lightly grease the sheet pan.
8. Arrange the bread slices into "Air Fry Basket" buttered side up and insert in the oven.
9. Serve warm.

Buttered Up Garlic and Fennel

PREPARATION
10 min

COOKING
2.5 min

SERVING
4

INGREDIENTS

- 1 and ½ pounds fennel bulbs, cut into wedges
- ¼ teaspoon dried dill weed
- 1/3 cup dry white wine
- ½ stick butter
- 2 garlic cloves, sliced
- ½ teaspoon cayenne
- 2/3 cup stock
- ½ teaspoon salt
- ¼ teaspoon ground black pepper

DIRECTIONS

1. Set your Ninja Foodi on Sauté mode
2. Then add butter, let it heat up
3. Add garlic and cook for 30 seconds
4. Add rest of the ingredients
5. Close the lid and cook on LOW pressure for 2 minutes
6. Remove the lid once done
7. Serve and enjoy!

Nuts Granola

PREPARATION
10 min

COOKING
90 min

SERVING
12

INGREDIENTS

- 1 cup raw pecans
- 1 cup raw almonds
- 1 cup raw walnuts
- 1½ teaspoons ground cinnamon
- ¼ cup Erythritol

DIRECTIONS

1. In the greased pot of Ninja Foodie, add all the ingredients and mix until well combined.
2. Close the Ninja Foodi with a crisping lid and select "Slow Cooker".
3. Set on "Low" for 1½-2 hours.
4. Press "Start/Stop" to begin cooking.
5. Move the granola onto an enormous heating sheet and set aside to cool completely before serving.

Roasted Garlic Potatoes

PREPARATION
5-10 min

COOKING
20 min

SERVING
4

INGREDIENTS

- 2 lb./ 900g baby potatoes, sliced into wedges
- 2 tablespoons olive oil
- 2 teaspoons garlic salt

DIRECTIONS

1. Toss the potatoes in olive oil and garlic salt. Add the potatoes to the Ninja Foodi basket. Seal the crisping lid. Set it to "Air Fry". Cook at 390° F / 200° C for 20 minutes.

Serving Suggestion:

Sprinkle dried herbs on top.

Bacon and Tomato Omelet

PREPARATION
10 min

COOKING
20 min

SERVING
4

INGREDIENTS

- 1 tablespoon cheddar, grated
- ¼ pound bacon, cooked and chopped
- 4 tomatoes, cubed
- 1 tablespoon parsley, chopped
- 1 tablespoon olive oil
- Salt and pepper to taste

DIRECTIONS

1. Take a small pan and place it over medium heat, add bacon and Sauté for 2 minutes until crisp
2. Take a bowl and add bacon, add remaining ingredients, and gently stir. Sprinkle cheese on top
3. Preheat Ninja Foodi by pressing the "Bake" option and setting it to 400° F / 205° C and timer to 10 minutes
4. Let it preheat until you hear a beep
5. Pour mixture into a baking dish and transfer baking dish inside Ninja Foodi, let it "Bake" for 8 minutes
6. Serve and enjoy!

Sausage & Bacon Omelet

PREPARATION
10 min

COOKING
10 min

SERVING
2

INGREDIENTS

- 4 eggs
- Ground black pepper, as required
- 1 bacon slice, chopped
- 2 sausages, chopped
- 1 onion, chopped
- 1 teaspoon fresh parsley, minced

DIRECTIONS

1. In a bowl, crack the eggs and black pepper and beat well.
2. Add the remaining ingredients and gently stir to combine.
3. Place the mixture into a baking pan.
4. Arrange the drip pan at the bottom of the Ninja Foodi cooking chamber.
5. Select "Air Fry" and then adjust the temperature to 320° F / 160° C.
6. Set the timer for 10 minutes and press the "Start".
7. When the display shows "Add Food", place the baking pan over the drip pan.
8. When the display shows "Turn Food", do nothing.
9. When cooking time is complete, remove the pan from the Ninja Foodi and serve warm.

Eggs in Avocado Cups

PREPARATION
10 min

COOKING
10 min

SERVING
2

INGREDIENTS

- avocado halved and pitted
- large eggs
- Salt and ground black pepper, as required
- cooked bacon slices, crumbled

DIRECTIONS

1. Carefully, scoop out about 2 teaspoons of fles from each avocado half.
2. Crack 1 egg in each avocado half and sprinkle with salt and black pepper.
3. Select "Bake/Roast" mode.
4. Press the Time button and again turn the dial to set the cooking time to 10 minutes.
5. Now push the Temp button and rotate the dial to set the temperature at 375° F / 190° C.
6. Press the "Start/Pause" button to start.
7. When the unit beeps to show that it is preheated, open the lid and line the "Sheet Pan" with a lightly, grease piece of foil.
8. Arrange avocado halves into the "Sheet Pan" and insert it in the oven.
9. Top each avocado half with bacon pieces and serve.

Chocolate Granola

PREPARATION
15 min

COOKING
120 min

SERVING
20

INGREDIENTS

- 5 cups unsweetened coconut, shredded 1 cup almonds, chopped
- 1/3 cups sunflowe seeds
- 1/3 cups pumpkin seeds
- ¼ cup cacao nibs
- 2½ ounces coconut oil, melted
- 3 tablespoons Erythritol
- 4 tablespoons cocoa powder unsweetened 1 tablespoon lemon zest, grated finely

DIRECTIONS

1. In the pot of Ninja Foodi, add all ingredients and mix well.
2. Close the Ninja Foodi with a crisping lid and select "Slow Cooker".
3. Set on "High" for 2 hours.
4. Press "Start/Stop" to begin cooking.
5. Stir the mixture after every 15 minutes.
6. Move the granola onto an enormous heating sheet and set aside to cool completely before serving.

Zucchini & Coconut Bread

PREPARATION
15 min

COOKING
180 min

SERVING
10

INGREDIENTS

- 2½ cups zucchini, shredded
- ½ teaspoon salt
- 1 1/3 cups almond flou
- 2/3 cup coconut, shredded
- 2 teaspoons ground cinnamon
- ½ teaspoon ground ginger
- ¼ teaspoon ground nutmeg
- 3 large organic eggs
- ¼ cup butter, melted
- ¼ cup water
- ½ teaspoon organic vanilla extract
- ½ cup walnuts, chopped

DIRECTIONS

1. Arrange a large sieve in a sink.
2. Place the zucchini in a sieve and sprinkle with salt. Set aside to drain for about 1 hour.
3. With your hands, squeeze out the moisture from zucchini.
4. In a large bowl, add the almond flour coconut, Erythritol, protein powder, baking powder, and spices and mix well.
5. Add the zucchini, eggs, coconut oil, water, and vanilla extract and mix until well combined.
6. Fold in the walnuts.
7. At the bottom of a greased Ninja Foodie, place the mixture.
8. Close the Ninja Foodi with a crisping lid and select "Slow Cook".
9. Set on "Low" for 2½-3 hours.
10. Press "Start/Stop" to begin cooking.
11. Keep the bread inside for about 5-10 minutes.
12. Carefully, remove the bread from the pot and place onto a wire rack to cool completely before slicing.
13. Cut the bread into desired-sized slices and serve.

Early Morning Kale And Sausage Delight

PREPARATION
10 min

COOKING
10 min

SERVING
4

INGREDIENTS

- Olive oil as needed
- 1 cup mushrooms
- 2 cups kale chopped
- 4 sausage links
- 4 medium eggs
- 1 medium yellow onion, sweet

DIRECTIONS

1. Open the lid of your Ninja Foodi and arrange the Reversible Rack

2. Preheat your Ninja Foodi to "High" and set the timer to 5 minutes

3. Once you hear the beeping sound, arrange sausages over the Reversible Rack

4. Cook for 2 minutes, fli and cook for 3 minutes more

5. Take a baking pan and spread out the kale, onion, mushroom, sausage and crack an egg on top

6. Cook on "Bake" mode on 350° F / 180° C for about 5 minutes more

7. Serve and enjoy!

Carrot Bread

PREPARATION
15 min

COOKING
180 min

SERVING
12

INGREDIENTS

- 1 cup almond flou
- 1/3 cup coconut flou
- 1½ teaspoons organic baking powder
- 1 teaspoon ground cinnamon
- ¼ teaspoon ground cloves
- ¼ teaspoon ground nutmeg
- ¼ teaspoon salt
- 1 cup Erythritol
- 1/3 cup coconut oil, softened
- 3 organic eggs
- 1 teaspoon organic vanilla extract
- ½ teaspoon organic almond extract
- 2 cups plus 2 tablespoons carrots, peeled and shredded

DIRECTIONS

1. In a bowl, add the flours baking powder, baking soda, spices, and salt and mix well.
2. In another large bowl, add the Erythritol, coconut oil, eggs, and both extracts and beat until well combined.
3. Add the flou mixture and mix until just combined.
4. Fold in the carrots.
5. Place the mixture into a greased 8x4-inch silicone bread pan.
6. Arrange a "Reversible Rack" in the pot of Ninja Foodi.
7. Place the pan over the "Reversible Rack".
8. Close the Ninja Foodi with a crisping lid and select "Slow Cook".
9. Set on "Low" for 3 hours.
10. Press "Start/Stop" to begin cooking.
11. Place the bread pan onto a wire rack for about 5-10 minutes.
12. Carefully, remove the bread from the pan and place it onto the wire rack to cool completely before slicing.
13. Cut the bread into desired-sized slices and serve.

CHAPTER 6

Breakfasts

Breakfast Burrito

PREPARATION
15 min

COOKING
40 min

SERVING
12

INGREDIENTS

- 1 teaspoon olive oil
- 1 lb. / 450g breakfast sausage
- 2 cups potatoes, diced
- Salt and pepper to taste
- 10 eggs, beaten
- 3 cups cheddar cheese, shredded
- 12 tortillas

DIRECTIONS

1. Pour olive oil into a pan over medium heat.
2. Cook potatoes and sausage for 7 to 10 minutes, stirring frequently.
3. Spread this mixture on the bottom of the Ninja Foodi pot.
4. Season with salt and pepper.
5. Pour the eggs and cheese on top.
6. Select the bake setting.
7. Cook at 325° F / 160° C for 20 minutes.
8. Top the tortilla with the cooked mixture and roll.
9. Sprinkle cheese on the top side.
10. Add the air fryer basket to the Ninja Foodi.
11. "Air Fry" the burrito at 375° F / 190° C for 10 minutes.

Serving Suggestions:

You can also serve this as a snack.

Tips:

The burrito can be made ahead and frozen. Take it out of the freezer 30 minutes before cooking it.

Breakfast Omelet

PREPARATION
15 min

COOKING
10 min

SERVING
6

INGREDIENTS

- 6 eggs
- 1 white onion, diced
- 1 red bell pepper, diced
- 6 mushrooms, chopped
- 2 slices ham, chopped and cooked
- 1 cup cheddar cheese, shredded
- Salt and pepper to taste

DIRECTIONS

1. Beat eggs in a bowl.
2. Stir in the rest of the ingredients.
3. Set your Ninja Foodi to "Air Fry".
4. Pour the egg mixture into the pot.
5. Cook at 390° F / 200° C for 10 minutes, stirring halfway through.

Serving Suggestions:

Serve with toasted garlic bread.

Tips:

You can also use turkey bacon to replace ham in this recipe.

Completely Stuffed Up Bacon And Pepper

PREPARATION
10 min

COOKING
15 min

SERVING
4

INGREDIENTS

- Chopped parsley, for garnish
- Salt and pepper to taste
- 4 whole large eggs
- 4 bell pepper, seeded and tops removed
- 4 slices bacon, cooked and chopped
- 1 cup cheddar cheese, shredded

DIRECTIONS

1. Take the bell pepper and divide the cheese and bacon evenly between them
2. Crack eggs into each of the bell pepper
3. Season the bell pepper with salt and pepper
4. Preheat your Ninja Food in "Air Fry" mode with temperature to 390° F / 200° C
5. Set timer to 15 minutes
6. Once you hear the beep, transfer the bell pepper to the cooking basket
7. Transfer your prepared pepper to Ninja Foodi and cook for 10-15 minutes until the eggs are cooked, and the yolks are just slightly runny
8. Garnish with a bit of parsley
9. Enjoy!

Roasted Breakfast Potatoes

PREPARATION
15 min

COOKING
25 min

SERVING
4

INGREDIENTS

- 3 large potatoes, diced
- 1 tablespoon olive oil
- 1 tablespoon butter
- Garlic salt and pepper to taste
- 3 sprigs thyme
- 2 sprigs rosemary

DIRECTIONS

1. Add potatoes to the Ninja Foodi pot.
2. Toss in olive oil and butter.
3. Season with garlic salt and pepper.
4. Top with the herb sprigs.
5. Seal the pot.
6. Set it to "Air Fry".
7. Cook at 375° F / 190° C for 25 minutes.

Serving Suggestions:

Garnish with chopped parsley.

Tips:

Stir the potatoes halfway through to ensure even cooking.

Bacon

PREPARATION
5 min

COOKING
10 min

SERVING
3

INGREDIENTS

- 6 slices bacon
- 2 tablespoons water

DIRECTIONS

1. Pour water to the bottom of the Ninja Foodi pot.
2. Place the "Reversible Rack" inside.
3. Put the bacon slices on the "Reversible Rack".
4. Select the "Air Fry" function.
5. Cook at 350° F / 180° C for 5 minutes per side or until golden and crispy.

Serving Suggestions:

Serve with bread and vegetables for a complete breakfast meal.

Tips:

Use turkey bacon if you want a breakfast dish that's lower in fat and cholesterol.

Healthy Potato Pancakes

PREPARATION
10 min

COOKING
24 min

SERVING
4

INGREDIENTS

- Salt and pepper to taste
- 3 tablespoons flou
- ¼ teaspoon salt
- ½ teaspoon garlic powder
- 2 tablespoons unsalted butter
- ¼ cup milk
- 1 egg, beaten
- 1 medium onion, chopped
- 4 medium potatoes, peeled and cleaned

DIRECTIONS

1. Take your potatoes and peel them well
2. Shred the potatoes and soak the shredded potatoes under cold water
3. Drain your potatoes in a colander
4. Take a separate bowl and add milk, eggs, butter, garlic powder, pepper, and salt. Add flou and mix the whole mixture well
5. Add shredded potatoes
6. Preheat your Ninja Foodi to "Air Fry" mode with a temperature of 390° F / 200° C, setting the timer to 24 minutes
7. Once you hear the beep, add ¼ cup of potato pancake batter to the cooking basket
8. Cook for 12 minutes until you have a nice golden texture
9. Repeat with remaining batter
10. Serve once done, enjoy!

French Toast

PREPARATION
15 min

COOKING
10 min

SERVING
4

INGREDIENTS

- 6 eggs
- 1 cup milk
- 1 cup heavy cream
- 1 teaspoon honey
- Cooking spray
- 1 loaf French bread, sliced
- 1/2 cup butter
- 1/2 cup sugar

DIRECTIONS

1. Beat the eggs in a bowl.
2. Stir in milk, cream, and honey.
3. Dip the bread slices into the mixture.
4. Place inside the Ninja Foodi.
5. Spread some butter and sprinkle sugar on top of the bread slices.
6. Seal the pot and "Air Fry" at 350° F / 180° C for 5 to 10 minutes.

Serving Suggestions:

Serve with maple syrup.

Tips:

It's a good idea to use day-old bread for this recipe.

Crispy Garlic Potatoes

PREPARATION
10 min

COOKING
20 min

SERVING
8

INGREDIENTS

- 1 1/2 lb. / 680g potatoes, diced
- 1 tablespoon avocado oil
- 1 teaspoon garlic powder
- Salt and pepper to taste

DIRECTIONS

1. Toss the potatoes in oil.
2. Season with garlic powder, salt, and pepper.
3. Add the "Reversible Rack" to the Ninja Foodi Grill.
4. Select an "Air Fry" setting.
5. Cook at 400° F / 200° C for 20 minutes, tossing halfway through.

Serving Suggestions:

Sprinkle with chopped turkey bacon crisps.

Tips:

You can also season the potatoes with paprika.

French Toast Sticks

PREPARATION
10 min

COOKING
10 min

SERVING
12

INGREDIENTS

- 5 eggs
- 1 cup almond milk
- 1/4 cup sugar
- 1 teaspoon vanilla extract
- 4 tablespoons melted butter
- 4 bread slices, sliced into 12 sticks

DIRECTIONS

1. Beat the eggs in a bowl.
2. Stir in milk, sugar, vanilla, and butter.
3. Dip the breadsticks into the mixture.
4. Add these to the "Reversible Rack" and place inside the Ninja Foodi.
5. "Air Fry" at 350° F / 180° C for 8 to 10 minutes.

Serving Suggestions:

Sprinkle with cinnamon powder before serving.

Tips:

Prepare in advance and freeze for later use.

CHAPTER 7

Easy Vegetarian and Vegan Recipes

Vegetable Fritters

PREPARATION
10 min

COOKING
15 min

SERVING
10

INGREDIENTS

- 3 tablespoons ground flaxsee   mixed with 1/2 cup water
- 2 potatoes, shredded
- 2 cups frozen mixed vegetables
- 1 cup frozen peas, thawed
- 1/2 cup onion, chopped
- 1/4 cup fresh cilantro, chopped
- 1/2 cup almond flou
- Salt to taste
- Cooking spray

DIRECTIONS

1. Combine all the ingredients in a bowl. Form patties. Spray each patty with oil.

2. Transfer to the Ninja Foodi basket. Set it to "Air Fry". Close the crisping lid.

3. Cook at 360° F / 180° C for 15 minutes, flippin   halfway through.

Tips:

You can also omit the cooking spray for an oil-free recipe.

Roasted Spicy Potatoes

PREPARATION
15 min

COOKING
25 min

SERVING
4

INGREDIENTS

- 1 lb. / 450g baby potatoes, sliced into wedges
- 2 tablespoons olive oil
- Salt to taste
- 1 tablespoon garlic powder
- 1 tablespoon paprika
- 1/2 cup mayonnaise
- 2 tablespoons white wine vinegar
- 2 tablespoons tomato paste
- 1 teaspoon chili powder

DIRECTIONS

1. Toss potatoes in oil.
2. Sprinkle it with salt, garlic powder, and paprika.
3. Add a crisper plate to the air fryer basket.
4. Add a basket to the Ninja Foodi.
5. Set it to "Air Fry".
6. Set it to 360° F / 180° C for 30 minutes.
7. Press start to preheat.
8. Put the potatoes on the crisper plate after 5 minutes.
9. Cook for 25 minutes.
10. While waiting, mix the remaining ingredients.
11. Toss potatoes in spicy mayo mixture and serve.

Serving Suggestions:

Sprinkle with chopped parsley before serving.

Tips:

Poke potatoes with a fork before roasting.

Garlic Pepper Potato Chips

PREPARATION
10 min

COOKING
10 min

SERVING
10

INGREDIENTS

- 1 large potato, sliced into thin chips
- Cooking spray
- Salt and garlic powder to taste
- 1 teaspoon black pepper

DIRECTIONS

1. Spray oil on the Ninja Foodi basket.
2. Season the potato with the salt, garlic powder, and black pepper.
3. Place potato chips on the basket. Seal the crisping lid. Set it to "Air Fry".
4. Cook at 450° F / 230° C for 10 minutes or until golden and crispy.

Serving Suggestion:

Serve with mayo dip.

Tips:

Press moisture out of the potatoes using a paper towel.

Brussels Sprouts

PREPARATION
10 min

COOKING
6 min

SERVING
10

INGREDIENTS

- 1 lb. / 450g Brussels sprouts
- 2 teaspoons olive oil
- 1/4 teaspoon garlic powder
- 1/4 teaspoon salt

DIRECTIONS

1. Put the Brussels sprouts in a bowl. Pour the olive oil into the bowl.
2. Season the sprouts with garlic powder and salt. Put the sprouts on the basket.
3. Seal the crisping lid. Set it to "Air Fry" function.
4. Cook at 370° F / 190° C for 6 minutes, flippin   halfway through.

Serving Suggestion:

Serve as a side dish to the main course.

Tips:

Trim the brown leaves of the Brussels sprouts.

Zucchini Parmesan Chips

PREPARATION
10 min

COOKING
8 min

SERVING
10

INGREDIENTS

- ½ tsp. paprika
- ½ C. grated parmesan cheese
- ½ C. Italian breadcrumbs
- 1 lightly beaten egg
- 2 thinly sliced zucchinis

DIRECTIONS

1. Use a very sharp knife or mandolin slicer to slice zucchini as thinly as you can—Pat off extra moisture.

2. Beat egg with a pinch of pepper and salt and a bit of water.

3. Combine paprika, cheese, and breadcrumbs in a bowl.

4. Dip slices of zucchini into the egg mixture and then into breadcrumb mixture. Press gently to coat.

5. Insert the Crisp Basket, and close the hood. Select "Air Fry", set the temperature to 350° F / 180° C, and set the time to 8 minutes. Select "Start/Stop" to begin preheating.

Air Frying

6. With olive oil cooking spray, mist coated zucchini slices. Place into your air fryer in a single layer. Set temperature to 350° F / 180° C, and set time to 8 minutes.

7. Sprinkle with salt and serve with salsa.

Mashed Cauliflower Delight

PREPARATION
10 min

COOKING
5 min

SERVING
4

INGREDIENTS

- 1 large head cauliflower chopped into large pieces
- 1 garlic cloves, minced
- 1 tablespoon ghee
- ½ cup cashew cream
- 2 teaspoons fresh chives, minced
- Salt and pepper to taste

DIRECTIONS

1. Add the pot to your Ninja Foodi and add water
2. Add steamer basket on top and add cauliflowe pieces
3. Close the lid
4. Cook for 5 minutes on "High"
5. Quick-release the pressure
6. Now add the remaining ingredients
7. Open the lid and use your blender to mash the cauliflowe
8. Blend until you get a smooth mixture
9. Serve and enjoy!

Cheesy Mashed Sweet Potato Cakes

PREPARATION
10 min

COOKING
average **60** min

SERVING
4

INGREDIENTS

- ¾ cup bread crumbs
- 4 sweet potatoes
- ½ cup onions
- 2 cup of grated mozzarella cheese
- ¼ cup fresh grated parmesan cheese
- 2 large cloves finel chopped
- 1 egg
- 2 tsp. finel   chopped parsley
- Salt and pepper to taste

DIRECTIONS

1. Line your baking sheet with foil. Wash, peel, and cut the sweet potatoes into 6 pieces. Arrange them inside the baking sheet and drizzle a small amount of oil on top before seasoning with salt and pepper.

2. Cover with a baking sheet and bake it for 45 minutes. Once cooked, transfer them into a mixing bowl and mash them well with a potato masher.

3. To the sweet potatoes in a bowl, add green onions, parmesan, mozzarella, garlic, egg, parsley, and bread crumbs. Mash and combine the mixture using the masher.

4. Put the remaining ¼ cup of the breadcrumbs in place. Scoop a tsp. of the mixture into your palm and form round patties around ½ and inch thick. Dredge your patties in the breadcrumbs to cover both sides and set them aside.

5. Heat a tablespoon of oil in a medium nonstick pan. When the oil is hot, begin to cook the patties in batches 4 or 5 per session and cook each side for 6 minutes until they turn golden brown. Using a spoon or spatula, fli   them. Add oil to prevent burning.

Italian Squash Meal

PREPARATION
5-10 min

COOKING
16 min

SERVING
4

INGREDIENTS

- 1 medium butternut squash, peeled, seeded, and cut into ½ inch slices
- 1 and ½ teaspoons oregano, dried
- 1 teaspoon dried thyme
- 1 tablespoon olive oil
- ½ teaspoon salt
- ¼ teaspoon black pepper

DIRECTIONS

1. Add slices alongside other ingredients into a mixing bowl
2. Mix them well
3. Preheat your Ninja Foodi by pressing the "Grill" option and setting it to "Med".
4. Set the timer to 16 minutes
5. Allow it to preheat until it beep
6. Arrange squash slices over the grill grate
7. Cook for 8 minutes
8. Flip and cook for 8 minutes more
9. Serve and enjoy!

Air Grilled Brussels

PREPARATION
5-10 min

COOKING
12 min

SERVING
4

INGREDIENTS

- 6 slices bacon, chopped
- 1 pound brussels sprouts, halved
- 2 tablespoons olive oil, extra virgin
- 1 teaspoon salt
- ½ teaspoon black pepper, ground

DIRECTIONS

1. Add Brussels, olive oil, salt, pepper, and bacon into a mixing bowl
2. Preheat Ninja Foodi by pressing the "Air Fry" option and setting it to 390° F / 200° C.
3. Set the timer to 12 minutes
4. Allow it to preheat until it beeps
5. Arrange Brussels over basket and lock lid
6. Cook for 6 minutes
7. Shake it and cook for 6 minutes more
8. Serve and enjoy!

Tofu, Broccoli, and Carrot

PREPARATION
10 min

COOKING
20 min

SERVING
4

INGREDIENTS

- 1 block tofu, sliced into cubes
- 1 tablespoon sesame oil
- 1 tablespoon soy sauce
- 3 tablespoons tapioca starch
- 2 carrots, sliced into strips
- 1 cup broccoli floret
- 2 tablespoons orange zest
- 1/2 cup orange juice
- 3 tablespoons rice vinegar
- 1 tablespoon light soy sauce
- 1 tablespoon chicken stock
- 2 tablespoons sugar
- 2 teaspoons cornstarch
- 2 cloves garlic, minced
- Salt to taste

DIRECTIONS

1. Coat the tofu with the sesame oil and soy sauce. Cover with tapioca starch.

2. Put the tofu cubes in the Ninja Foodi basket. Seal the crisping lid.

3. Press "Air Fry". Cook at 390° F / 200° C for 5 minutes. Stir the tofu and cook for another 5 minutes. Take the tofu out of the pot. Mix the rest of the ingredients.

4. Set the pot to sauté. Add the broccoli and carrots with the mixture.

5. Put the tofu back. Simmer for 10 minutes.

Serving Suggestion:

Serve with a bowl of hot rice.

Tips:

You can also fry the broccoli and carrots if you like them crispy.

Garlic and Swiss Chard Garlic

PREPARATION
10 min

COOKING
7 min

SERVING
4

INGREDIENTS

- 4 bacon slices, chopped
- 1 bunch Swiss chard, chopped
- 2 tablespoons ghee
- ½ teaspoon garlic paste
- 3 tablespoons lemon juice
- ½ cup chicken stock
- Salt and pepper to taste

DIRECTIONS

1. Set your Ninja Foodi to "Sauté" mode
2. Then add bacon, stir well
3. Cook for a few minutes
4. Add ghee, lemon juice, garlic paste
5. Then give a gentle stir
6. Add Swiss chard, salt, pepper, and stock
7. Close the lid
8. Cook on "High" pressure for 3 minutes
9. Quick-release the pressure
10. Serve and enjoy!

Fried Tempeh

PREPARATION
10 min

COOKING
20 min

SERVING
10

INGREDIENTS

- 0.45 lb. / 200g tempeh, sliced into chunks
- 2 tablespoons vegan mayonnaise
- 3 tablespoons bread crumbs
- Sauce:
- 2 tablespoons Korean red pepper paste
- 2 cloves garlic, crushed
- 1 tablespoon maple syrup
- 1 tablespoon soy sauce
- 1 tablespoon water
- Salt and pepper to taste

DIRECTIONS

1. Put the mayo in one bowl and the breadcrumbs in another. Dilute the mayo with water. Coat each tempeh with mayo and then with the breadcrumbs.

2. Place in the Ninja Foodi basket. Seal the crisping lid. Set it to "Air Fry".

3. Cook at 350° F / 180° C for 15 minutes or until golden and crispy.

4. Stir every 5 minutes. Take them out and set aside.

5. Mix all the sauce ingredients. Put in the pot. Set it to sauté. Simmer for 5 minutes. Add the tempeh to the sauce and toss to coat evenly.

Serving Suggestion:

Top with sesame seeds.

Tips:

Cook in batches for even browning.

Hearty Lemon Green Beans

PREPARATION
15 min

COOKING
12 min

SERVING
4

INGREDIENTS

- 1 lb. / 450g green beans, trimmed
- 1 tablespoon butter, melted
- 1 tablespoon fresh lemon juice
- ¼ teaspoon garlic powder
- Salt and pepper to taste
- ½ teaspoon lemon zest, grated

DIRECTIONS

1. Take a large-sized bowl and add all listed ingredients, except lemon zest
2. Toss and coat well
3. Press "Power Button" on your Air Fryer and select "Air Fry" mode
4. Press the Time Button and set the time to 12 minutes
5. Push Temp Button and set temp to 400° F / 200° C
6. Press the "Start/Pause" button and start the device
7. Arrange the green beans into the "Reversible Rack" and push into the oven, let it cook until the timer runs out
8. Serve warm with a lemon zest garnish!

Cheddar Cauliflower Bowl

PREPARATION
10 min

COOKING
15 min

SERVING
8

INGREDIENTS

- 1/4 cup butter
- 1/2 sweet onion, chopped
- 1 head cauliflower chopped
- 4 cups herbed vegetable stock
- 1/2 teaspoon ground nutmeg
- 1 cup heavy whip cream
- Salt and pepper as needed
- 1 cup cheddar cheese, shredded

DIRECTIONS

1. Set your Ninja Foodi to "Sauté" mode and add butter, let it heat up and melt

2. Add onion and Cauliflower sauté for 10 minutes until tender and lightly browned

3. Add vegetable stock and nutmeg, bring to a boil

4. Lock lid and cook on "High" pressure for 5 minutes, quick release pressure once done

5. Remove the pot and from Foodi and stir in heavy cream, puree using an immersion blender

6. Season with more salt and pepper and serve with a topping of cheddar. Enjoy!

Grilled Cauliflower Steak

PREPARATION
30 min

COOKING
22 min

SERVING
2

INGREDIENTS

- 2 cauliflowe steaks
- 1/4 cup vegetable oil, divided
- Salt and pepper to taste
- 1 onion, chopped
- 3 cloves garlic, minced
- 1/4 cup Kalamata olives, chopped
- 1 tablespoon fresh parsley, chopped
- 1 tablespoon fresh oregano, chopped
- 1/2 lb. /225g feta cheese, crumbled
- 1 tablespoon lemon juice
- 1/4 cup walnuts, chopped

DIRECTIONS

1. Add a grill grate to your Ninja Foodi.
2. Choose a "Grill" setting.
3. Set it to the max for 17 minutes.
4. Press start to preheat.
5. Brush both sides of cauliflowe steaks with oil.
6. Season with salt and pepper.
7. Grill for 10 minutes per side.
8. Mix the remaining ingredients in a bowl.
9. Spread mixture on top of the steaks and cook for another 2 minutes.

Serving Suggestions:

Serve as a vegetarian main dish.

Tips:

Use ricotta cheese in place of feta if not available.

Coconut Cabbage

PREPARATION
10 min

COOKING
around 8 min

SERVING
4

INGREDIENTS

- 1/2 cup cabbage, shredded
- 1 oz. / 30g dry coconut
- 3 large whole eggs
- 3 large egg yolks
- 1/3 medium carrot, sliced
- ½ oz. / 15g yellow onion, sliced
- 1 teaspoon turmeric powder
- 2 tablespoons lemon juice
- 1/3 cup water
- 3 tablespoons olive oil
- ½ tablespoon mustard powder
- ½ teaspoon mild curry powder
- 1 large garlic cloves, diced
- 1 and ½ teaspoons salt

DIRECTIONS

1. Set your Ninja Foodi to "Sauté" mode
2. Add oil, stir in onions, salt
3. Cook for 4 minutes
4. Stir in spices, garlic, and Sauté for 30 seconds
5. Stir in the rest of the ingredients and close the lid
6. Cook on "High" pressure for 3 minutes
7. Naturally, release the pressure over 10 minutes
8. Serve and enjoy!

Roasted Mixed Veggies

PREPARATION
15 min

COOKING
15 min

SERVING
4

INGREDIENTS

- 1 zucchini, sliced
- 8 oz. / 225g mushrooms, sliced
- 2 tablespoons olive oil
- 1 tablespoon garlic, minced
- 1 teaspoon onion powder
- 1 teaspoon garlic powder
- Salt and pepper to taste

DIRECTIONS

1. Choose an "Air Fry" setting in your Ninja Foodi.
2. Insert Crisp basket.
3. Preheat it to 390° F / 200° C.
4. Toss zucchini and mushrooms in oil.
5. Sprinkle it with garlic.
6. Season with onion powder, garlic powder, salt, and pepper.
7. Place in the basket.
8. Cook for 10 minutes.
9. Stir and cook for another 5 minutes.

Serving Suggestions:

Serve as a side dish to the main course.

Tips:

Do not overcrowd the basket with veggies.

Roast Carrot and Cumin

PREPARATION
15 min

COOKING
12 min

SERVING
4

INGREDIENTS

- 20 oz. / 570g carrots, peeled
- 1 tablespoon olive oil
- 1 teaspoon cumin seeds
- Handful fresh coriander

DIRECTIONS

1. Preheat Ninja Foodi by pressing the "Air Fry" option and setting it to 350° F / 180° C and timer to 12 minutes
2. Let it preheat until you hear a beep
3. Take a mixing bowl and add oil, honey, and carrots
4. Give it a nice stir and make sure that they are coated well
5. Season with some dill, pepper, and salt
6. Transfer the mix to your Ninja Foodi and cook for 12 minutes and enjoy it!

Simple Asparagus

PREPARATION
10 min

COOKING
10 min

SERVING
3

INGREDIENTS

- 1 lb. / 450g fresh thick asparagus, trimmed
- 1 tablespoon olive oil
- Salt and ground black pepper, as required

DIRECTIONS

1. In a bowl, add all the ingredients and toss to coat well.
2. Arrange the asparagus onto a cooking tray.
3. Arrange the drip pan at the bottom of the Ninja Foodi cooking chamber.
4. Select "Air Fry" and then adjust the temperature to 350° F / 180° C.
5. Set the timer for 10 minutes and press the "Start."
6. When the display shows "Add Food" insert the cooking tray in the center position.
7. When the display shows "Turn Food," turn the asparagus.
8. When cooking time is complete, remove the tray from Ninja Foodi and serve hot.

Veggie Hash

PREPARATION
10 min

COOKING
9 min

SERVING
4

INGREDIENTS

- 1 cup cauliflower chopped
- ½ cup spinach, chopped
- ½ cup dark leaf kale, chopped
- 6 whole eggs
- 3 teaspoons coconut oil
- 2 garlic cloves
- 1 teaspoon mustard
- 1 tablespoon lemon juice
- ½ teaspoon salt
- ½ teaspoon pepper

DIRECTIONS

1. Set your Ninja Foodi to "Sauté" mode
2. Add coconut oil, add garlic, cook until fragrant
3. Then add chopped cauliflowe
4. Cook for 5 minutes
5. Stir in all ingredients except eggs, cook for 2 minutes
6. Stir in eggs, close the lid
7. Cook for 2 minutes on "High" pressure
8. Quick-release the pressure
9. Serve and enjoy!

Veggie Lasagna

PREPARATION
30 min

COOKING
45 min

SERVING
8

INGREDIENTS

- 6 cups tomato sauce
- 2 tablespoons olive oil
- 2 cloves garlic, minced
- 1 teaspoon dried basil
- 1 teaspoon dried oregano
- Salt and pepper to taste
- 1 red bell pepper, chopped
- 1 green bell pepper, chopped
- 1 cup mushrooms, diced
- 1 cup broccoli, diced
- 1 eggplant, diced
- 4 cups mozzarella cheese
- 4 cups cream
- 1 pack lasagna pasta sheets

DIRECTIONS

1. Combine all ingredients except cheese, cream, and pasta sheets.
2. In another bowl, mix cheese and cream.
3. Spread some of the tomato sauce and veggie mixture on the bottom of the pot.
4. Top with the pasta sheets.
5. Spread another layer of the tomato sauce mixture, and then the cheese mixture.
6. Top with another layer of pasta sheets.
7. Repeat layers until all ingredients have been used.
8. Cover the top layer with foil.
9. Choose "Bake" setting.
10. Cook at 350° F / 180° C for 45 minutes.

Serving Suggestions:

Sprinkle with Parmesan and basil before serving.

Tips:

You can also pre-boil the lasagna sheets and vegetables to reduce cooking time in the Ninja Foodi.

Cheddar Cauliflower Meal

PREPARATION
10-15 min

COOKING
15 min

SERVING
2

INGREDIENTS

- ½ teaspoon garlic powder
- ½ teaspoon paprika
- Ocean salt and ground dark pepper to taste
- 1 head cauliflower stemmed and leaves removed
- 1 cup Cheddar cheese, shredded
- Ranch dressing, for garnish
- ¼ cup canola oil or vegetable oil
- 2 tablespoons chopped chives
- 4 slices bacon, cooked and crumbled

DIRECTIONS

1. Cut the cauliflowe into 2 inch / 5 cm pieces.
2. In a blending bowl, including the oil, garlic powder, and paprika. Season with salt and ground dark pepper; join well. Coat the floret with the blend.
3. Take Ninja Foodi, mastermind it over your kitchen stage, and open the top cover.
4. Mastermind the flam broil mesh and close the top cover.
5. Press "Broil" and select at "Max". Set to 15 minutes and afterward press "Start/Stop" Ninja Foodi will begin preheating.
6. Ninja Foodi is preheated and prepared to cook when it begins to signal. After you hear a blare, open the top.
7. Organize the pieces over the flam broil grind.
8. Close the top lid and cook for 10 minutes. Now open the top lid, fli the pieces and top with the cheese.
9. Close the top lid and cook for 5 more minutes. Serve warm with the chives and ranch dressing on top.

Buttery Spinach Meal

PREPARATION
10 min

COOKING
15 min

SERVING
4

INGREDIENTS

- 2/3 cup Kalamata olives, halved and pitted
- 1 and ½ cups feta cheese, grated
- 4 tablespoons butter
- 2 lb. / 900g spinach, chopped and boiled
- Pepper and salt to taste
- 4 teaspoons lemon zest, grated

DIRECTIONS

1. Take a mixing bowl and add spinach, butter, salt, pepper and mix well
2. Preheat Ninja Foodi by pressing the "Air Fry" option and setting it to 340° F / 170° C and timer to 15 minutes
3. Let it preheat until you hear a beep
4. Arrange a reversible trivet in the "Crisp Basket" and add spinach mixture
5. Let them cook until the timer runs out
6. Serve and enjoy!

Grilled Veggies

PREPARATION
30 min

COOKING
10 min

SERVING
4

INGREDIENTS

- 1 onion, sliced
- 1 red bell pepper, sliced
- 1 cup button mushrooms, sliced
- 1 zucchini, sliced
- 1 eggplant, sliced
- 1 cup asparagus, trimmed and sliced
- 1 squash, sliced
- 2 tablespoons olive oil
- Salt and pepper to taste

DIRECTIONS

1. Install a grill grate to your Ninja Foodi.

2. Select the "Grill" setting.

3. Preheat it to "Medium" for 10 minutes.

4. Toss the veggies in olive oil and season with salt and pepper.

5. Add to the grill grate.

6. Grill for 10 minutes.

Serving Suggestions:

Sprinkle with dried herbs before serving.

Tips:

It's better to serve this dish at room temperature.

Vegetarian Bowl

PREPARATION
20 min

COOKING
25 min

SERVING
4

INGREDIENTS

- 3 cups tofu, sliced into cubes
- 1 cup red bell pepper, sliced into strips
- 1 cup yellow bell pepper, sliced into strips
- 1 cup mushroom, sliced
- 1/4 white onion, chopped
- Cooking spray
- Garlic salt to taste
- 4 cups cooked brown rice

DIRECTIONS

1. Select "Air Fry" setting in your Ninja Foodi.
2. Spray tofu cubes with oil.
3. Add tofu cubes to the "Crisp Basket".
4. Cook at 390° F / 200° C for 10 minutes or until crispy.
5. Transfer to a plate.
6. Toss veggies in a bowl.
7. Spray with oil and season with garlic salt.
8. Cook at 390° F / 200° C for 10 minutes, shaking the basket halfway through
9. Add brown rice to serving bowls.
10. Top with the crispy tofu and vegetables.

Serving Suggestions:

Sprinkle with chopped scallions before serving.

Tips:

You can also use meat in place of tofu for this recipe if you prefer.

CHAPTER 8

Easy Chicken And Poultry Recipes

Excellent Chicken Tomatino

PREPARATION
10 min

COOKING
12 min

SERVING
4

INGREDIENTS

- ½ teaspoon salt
- 1 garlic clove, minced
- 2 tablespoons olive oil
- ¾ cup vinegar
- 8 plum tomatoes
- ¼ cup fresh basil leaves
- 4 chicken breast, boneless and skinless

DIRECTIONS

1. Take your fin food processor and add olive oil, vinegar, salt, garlic, and basil. Blend the mixture well until you have a smooth texture
2. Add tomatoes and blend once again
3. Take a mixing bowl and add tomato mix, chicken and mix well
4. Let the mixture chill for 1-2 hours
5. Preheat your Ninja Foodi to "High" and set the timer to 6 minutes
6. Once you hear the beep, arrange your prepared chicken over the "Reversible Rack"
7. Cook for 3 minutes more
8. Flip the chicken and cook for 3 minutes more
9. Once properly cooked, serve and enjoy!

Chicken Bean Bake

PREPARATION
8 min

COOKING
17 min

SERVING
8

INGREDIENTS

- ½ red onion, diced
- ½ red bell pepper, diced
- 1 tablespoon extra-virgin olive oil
- 2 (8 oz. / 225g) boneless, skinless chicken breasts cut into 1-inch cubes
- 1 cup white rice
- 1 (15 oz. / 425g) can corn, rinsed
- 1 (10 oz. / 285g) can roasted tomatoes with chiles
- 1 (15 oz. / 425g) can black beans, rinsed and drained
- 1 (1 oz. / 30g) packet taco seasoning
- 2 cups shredded Cheddar cheese
- 2 cups chicken broth
- Kosher salt
- Black pepper (ground)

DIRECTIONS

1. Put in the chicken and mix for about 2-3 minutes to brown evenly.

2. Add the onion and bell pepper, stir-cook until softened for 2 minutes. Add the rice, tomatoes, beans, corn, taco seasoning, broth, salt, and pepper, combine well.

3. Seal the multi-cooker by locking it with the pressure lid; ensure to keep the pressure release valve locked/sealed.

4. Select "Pressure" mode and select the "High" pressure level. Then after, set the timer to 7 minutes and press "Start/Stop," it will start the cooking process by building up inside pressure.

5. When the timer goes off quickly release pressure by adjusting the pressure valve to "Vent", after pressure gets released, open the pressure lid. Add the cheese on top.

6. Seal the multi-cooker by locking it with the Crisping Lid; ensure to keep the pressure release valve locked/sealed.

7. Select "Broil" mode and select the "High" pressure level. Then after, set the timer to 8 minutes and press "Start/Stop," it will start the cooking process by building up inside pressure.

8. When the timer goes off quickly release pressure by adjusting the pressure valve to "Vent", after pressure gets released, open the Crisping Lid.

Feisty Hot Pepper Wings Delight

PREPARATION
7 min

COOKING
25 min

SERVING
4

INGREDIENTS

- ½ cup hot pepper sauce
- 2 tablespoons butter, melted
- 1 tablespoon coconut oil
- 1 lb. / 450g chicken wings
- 1 tablespoon ranch salad dressing
- ½ teaspoon paprika

DIRECTIONS

1. Take a bowl and add chicken, oil, ranch dressing, and paprika. Transfer to your fridge and let it chill for about 30-60 minutes
2. Take another bowl and add the pepper sauce alongside butter
3. Preheat your Ninja Foodi in "Med" temperature, with timer set to 25 minutes
4. Arrange the chicken wings over the "Reversible Rack"
5. Cook for 25 minutes
6. Serve once done with the pepper sauce
7. Enjoy!

Moroccan Roast Chicken

PREPARATION
10 min

COOKING
23 min

SERVING
4

INGREDIENTS

- 3 tablespoons plain yogurt
- 4 skinless, boneless chicken thighs
- 4 garlic cloves, chopped
- ½ teaspoon salt
- 1/3 cup olive oil
- ½ teaspoon fresh flat-lea parsley, chopped
- 2 teaspoons ground cumin
- 2 teaspoons paprika
- ¼ teaspoon crushed red pepper flake

DIRECTIONS

1. Take your food processor and add garlic, yogurt, salt, oil and blend well
2. Take a mixing bowl and add chicken, red pepper flakes paprika, cumin, parsley, garlic, and mix well
3. Let it marinate for 2-4 hours
4. Preheat Ninja Foodi by pressing the "Roast" option and setting it to 400° F / 200° C and timer to 23 minutes
5. Let it preheat until you hear a beep
6. Arrange chicken directly inside your cooking pot and lock lid, cook for 15 minutes, fli   and cook for the remaining time
7. Serve and enjoy with yogurt dip!

Shredded Salsa Chicken

PREPARATION
5 min

COOKING
20 min

SERVING
4

INGREDIENTS

- 1 lb. / 450g chicken breast, skin and bones removed
- 1 cup chunky salsa Keto friendly
- ½ teaspoon salt
- Pinch of oregano
- ¾ teaspoon cumin
- Pepper to taste

DIRECTIONS

1. Season chicken with all the listed spices, then add to Ninja Foodi
2. Cover with salsa and close the lid
3. Cook on "High" pressure for 20 minutes
4. Quick-release the pressure
5. Add chicken to a platter then shred the chicken
6. Serve and enjoy!

Hassel Back Chicken

PREPARATION
5 min

COOKING
60 min

SERVING
4

INGREDIENTS

- 8 large chicken breasts
- 2 cups fresh mozzarella cheese, thinly sliced
- 4 large Roma tomatoes, thinly sliced
- 4 tablespoons butter
- Salt and pepper to taste

DIRECTIONS

1. Add chicken breasts, season with salt and pepper to make deep slits
2. Stuff with mozzarella cheese slices and tomatoes in your chicken slits
3. Grease Ninja Foodi pot with butter
4. Arrange stuffe chicken breasts
5. Close the lid and "Bake/Roast" for 1 hour at 365° F / 185° C
6. Serve and enjoy!

Lemon And Chicken Extravaganza

PREPARATION
5 min

COOKING
24 min

SERVING
4

INGREDIENTS

- 4 bone-in, skin-on chicken thighs
- Salt and pepper to taste
- 2 tablespoons butter, divided
- 2 teaspoons garlic, minced
- 1/2 cup herbed chicken stock
- 1/2 cup heavy whip cream
- 1/2 a lemon, juiced

DIRECTIONS

1. Season your chicken thighs generously with salt and pepper
2. Set your Foodi to "Sauté" mode and add oil, let it heat up
3. Add thigh, Sauté both sides for 6 minutes. Remove thigh to a platter and keep it on the side
4. Add garlic, cook for 2 minutes. Whisk in chicken stock, heavy cream, lemon juice and gently stir
5. Bring the mix to a simmer and reintroduce chicken
6. Lock lid and cook for 10 minutes on "High" pressure
7. Release pressure over 10 minutes. Serve and enjoy!

Baked Coconut Chicken

PREPARATION
10 min

COOKING
13 min

SERVING
4

INGREDIENTS

- 2 large eggs
- 2 teaspoons garlic powder
- 1 teaspoon salt
- ½ teaspoon ground black pepper
- ¾ cup Coconut Aminos
- 1 lb. / 450g chicken tenders
- Cooking spray as needed

DIRECTIONS

1. Preheat Ninja Foodi by squeezing the "Air Fry" alternative and setting it to 400° F / 200° C and timer to 13 minutes

2. Take a large-sized baking sheet and spray it with cooking spray

3. Take a wide dish and add garlic powder, eggs, pepper, and salt

4. Whisk well until everything is combined

5. Add the almond meal and coconut and mix well

6. Take your chicken tenders and dip them in the egg followed by dipping in the coconut mix

7. Shake off any excess

8. Transfer them to your Ninja Foodi and spray the tenders with a bit of oil.

9. Cook for 13 minutes until you have a nice golden-brown texture

10. Enjoy!

Barbecue Chicken

PREPARATION
4 min

COOKING
10 min

SERVING
4

INGREDIENTS

- 1 tablespoon olive oil
- 3 chicken breasts (boneless and skinless)
- 1 teaspoon garlic powder
- Salt and pepper to taste
- 1 cup barbecue sauce
- 1/2 cup water

DIRECTIONS

1. Pour the olive oil into the Ninja Foodi. Add the rest of the ingredients. Mix well.
2. Pour the barbecue sauce over the chicken. Do not stir. Seal the pot.
3. Set it to pressure. Cook at "High" pressure for 10 minutes.
4. Release the pressure naturally. Shred the chicken meat and toss in barbecue sauce.

Serving Suggestion:

Serve with steamed vegetables.

Tips:

Use low sodium barbecue sauce.

Chicken Chili and Beans

PREPARATION
10 min

COOKING
15 min

SERVING
4

INGREDIENTS

- 1 ¼ lb. / 570g chicken breast, cut into pieces
- 1 can corn
- ¼ teaspoon garlic powder
- 1 can black beans, drained and rinsed
- 1 tablespoon oil
- 2 tablespoons chili powder
- 1 bell pepper, chopped
- ¼ teaspoon garlic powder
- ¼ teaspoon salt

DIRECTIONS

1. Preheat Ninja Foodi by squeezing the "Air Fry" alternative and setting it to 360° F / 180° C and timer to 15 minutes

2. Place all the ingredients in your Ninja Foodi cooking basket/alternatively, you may use a dish to mix the ingredients and then put the dish in the cooking basket

3. Stir to mix well

4. Cook for 15 minutes

5. Serve and enjoy!

Lemon Chicken with Garlic

PREPARATION
5 min

COOKING
14 min

SERVING
4

INGREDIENTS

- 6 chicken thighs
- Salt and pepper to taste
- 1/2 teaspoon red chili flake
- 1/2 teaspoon garlic powder
- 1/2 teaspoon smoked paprika
- 2 tablespoons olive oil
- 3 tablespoons butter
- 1 onion, chopped
- 4 cloves garlic, minced
- 1 tablespoon lemon juice
- 1/4 cup low sodium broth
- 2 teaspoons Italian seasoning
- Lemon zest
- 2 tablespoons heavy cream

DIRECTIONS

1. Sprinkle the chicken thighs with salt, pepper, chili flakes garlic powder, and paprika.
2. Set the Ninja Foodi to "Sauté". Add the olive oil.
3. Cook the chicken for 3 minutes per side. Remove from the pot and set aside.
4. Melt the butter in the pot. Add the onion and garlic. Deglaze the pot with the lemon juice. Cook for 1 minute. Add the chicken broth, seasoning, and lemon zest.
5. Set the pot to "Pressure". Seal it. Cook at high pressure for 7 minutes.
6. Release the pressure naturally. Stir in the heavy cream before serving.

Serving Suggestion:

Garnish with fresh parsley.

Tips:

You can also use chicken breasts and slice horizontally.

Chicken Cacciatore

PREPARATION
4 min

COOKING
32 min

SERVING
4

INGREDIENTS

- 4 chicken thighs
- 2 tablespoons olive oil
- 1/2 onion, chopped
- 2 cloves garlic, minced
- 3 stalks celery, chopped
- 4 oz. / 115g mushrooms
- 14 oz. / 400g stewed tomatoes
- 2 teaspoons herbs de Provence
- 3/4 cup water
- 3 cubes chicken bouillon, crumbled
- 2 tablespoons tomato paste

DIRECTIONS

1. Set the Ninja Foodi to "Sauté". Add the oil and chicken.
2. Cook the chicken for 6 minutes per side. Remove the chicken and set aside.
3. Add the onion, garlic, celery, and mushrooms. Cook for 5 minutes, stirring frequently.
4. Put the chicken back. Pour in the tomatoes and tomato paste.
5. Add the rest of the ingredients. Seal the pot.
6. Set it to "Pressure". Cook at "High" pressure for 15 minutes. Release the pressure quickly.

Serving Suggestion:

Serve with pasta or rice.

Tips:

Add red pepper flake if you like the dish spicy.

Classic Honey Soy Chicken

PREPARATION
8 min

COOKING
17 min

SERVING
4

INGREDIENTS

- 4 boneless, skinless chicken bosoms cut into little pieces
- 4 garlic cloves, smashed
- 1 onion, diced
- ½ cup honey
- 2 tablespoon lime juice
- 2 teaspoon sesame oil
- 3 tablespoon soy sauce
- 1 tablespoon water
- 1 tablespoon cornstarch
- 1 teaspoon rice vinegar
- Black pepper and salt to taste

DIRECTIONS

1. In a mixing bowl, add the honey, sesame oil, lime juice, soy sauce, and rice vinegar. Combine well.
2. Seal the multi-cooker by locking it with the pressure lid; ensure to keep the pressure release valve locked/sealed.
3. Select "Pressure" mode and select the "High" pressure level. Then, set the timer to 15 minutes and press "Start/Stop"; it will start the cooking process by building up inside pressure.
4. At the point when the clock goes off brisk discharge pressure by adjusting the pressure valve to "Vent". After pressure gets released, open the pressure lid.
5. In a bowl, mix water and cornstarch until well dissolved.
6. Select "Sear/Sauté" mode and select the "Med" pressure level; add the cornstarch mixture in the pot and combine it, stir-cook for 2 minutes.
7. Serve warm.

Mexican Chicken Soup

PREPARATION
5-10 min

COOKING
14 min

SERVING
6

INGREDIENTS

- 1 (14.5 oz. / 410g) can black beans, rinsed and drained
- 14 oz. / 400g canned whole tomatoes, chopped
- 2 cups corn kernels
- ¼ cup cheddar cheese, shredded
- 5 chicken thighs, boneless, skinless
- 5 cups chicken broth
- 1 tablespoon ground cumin
- ½ teaspoon dried oregano
- 2 tablespoon tomato puree
- 1 tablespoon chili powder
- 3 cloves garlic, minced
- 2 stemmed jalapeno peppers, cored and chopped
- Fresh cilantro, chopped to garnish

DIRECTIONS

1. In the pot, add the chicken, chicken stock, cumin, oregano, garlic, tomato puree, tomatoes, chili powder, and jalapeno peppers; stir the mixture.

2. Seal the multi-cooker by locking it with the pressure lid; ensure to keep the pressure release valve locked/sealed.

3. Select "Pressure" mode and select the "High" pressure level. Then, set the timer to 10 minutes and press "Start/Stop"; it will start the cooking process by building up inside pressure.

4. At the point when the clock goes off brisk discharge pressure by adjusting the pressure valve to "Vent". After pressure gets released, open the pressure lid.

5. Shred the chicken and include it back in the pot.

6. Select "Sear/Sauté" mode and select "Md:Hi" pressure level; add the beans and corn and combine, stir-cook for 4 minutes.

7. Add the cilantro and cheese on top; serve warm.

Chicken Marsala

PREPARATION
10 min

COOKING
25 min

SERVING
4

INGREDIENTS

- 4 chicken breasts, sliced into strips
- 1 teaspoon garlic powder
- Salt and pepper to taste
- 1/2 cup all-purpose flou
- 3 tablespoons butter
- 3 tablespoons olive oil
- 3 cloves garlic, minced
- 1 shallot, sliced thinly
- 8 oz. / 225g mushrooms
- 2/3 cup Marsala wine
- 2/3 cup chicken stock
- 1/2 cup heavy cream

DIRECTIONS

1. Season the chicken with garlic powder, salt, and pepper. Coat the chicken with flour
2. Place the chicken on the Ninja Foodi basket. Put the basket inside the pot.
3. Seal the crisping lid. Set it to "Air Fry". Cook at 375° F / 190° C for 15 minutes.
4. Remove and set aside. Set the pot to "Sauté". Add the butter and oil.
5. Cook the garlic, shallot, and mushrooms. Pour in the wine and chicken broth.
6. Simmer for 10 minutes. Stir in the heavy cream.
7. Toss the chicken into the mixture. Serve.

Serving Suggestion:

Garnish with chopped parsley.

Tips:

Use whole wheat flour

Turkey Cream Noodles

PREPARATION
5 min

COOKING
35 min

SERVING
4

INGREDIENTS

- 8 oz. / 225g cremini mushrooms, sliced
- 1 can (10.5 oz. / 300g) cream of celery soup
- 2 tablespoons butter
- 1 lb. / 450g ground turkey
- 16 oz. / 450g peas
- 1 cup sour cream
- ¾ cup grated Parmesan cheese
- 4 cups chicken stock
- 1 (10 oz. / 280g) package egg noodles
- Kosher salt
- Freshly ground black pepper

DIRECTIONS

1. In the pot, add the butter; Select "Sear/Sauté" mode and select "Md: Hi" pressure level. Press "Start/Stop" After about 4 minutes, the butter will melt.

2. Add the mushrooms, turkey, and stir-cook for about 8 minutes to brown evenly.

3. Add the condensed soup and stock; stir and simmer for 15 minutes.

4. Add the egg noodles and peas; stir-cook for 8-10 minutes until the noodles are cooked well.

5. Add the sour cream and Parmesan cheese; stir the mixture, season with salt and pepper.

Turkey Bean Chili

PREPARATION
12 min

COOKING
average **30** min

SERVING
4

INGREDIENTS

- 2 garlic cloves, minced
- 1 ½ lb. / 680g turkey, ground
- 1 tablespoon extra-virgin olive oil
- 1 onion, chopped
- 1 tablespoon oregano, dried
- 1 tablespoon ground cumin
- 3 cans (15 oz. / 425g) of cannellini beans, rinsed and drained
- ⅛ teaspoon sea salt
- ⅛ teaspoon black pepper, freshly ground
- 4 cups chicken broth
- 1 pack biscuits

DIRECTIONS

1. In the pot, add the oil; Select "Sear/Sauté" mode and select "Md: Hi" pressure level.
2. Press "Start/Stop." After about 4-5 minutes, the oil will start simmering.
3. Add the onions, garlic, and cook (while stirring) for 2-3 minutes until they become softened and translucent.
4. Add the turkey, cumin, oregano, beans, broth, salt, and black pepper; stir the mixture.
5. Seal the multi-cooker by locking it with the pressure lid; ensure to keep the pressure release valve locked/sealed.
6. Select "Pressure" mode and select the "High" pressure level. Then, set the timer to 10 minutes and press "Start/Stop"; it will start the cooking process by building up inside pressure.
7. At the point when the clock goes off speedy discharge pressure by adjusting the pressure valve to "Vent". After pressure gets released, open the pressure lid.
8. Arrange the biscuits in a single layer over the mixture.
9. Seal the multi-cooker by locking it with the crisping lid; ensure to keep the pressure release valve locked/sealed.
10. Select "Broil" mode and select the "High" pressure level. Then, set the timer to 15 minutes and press "Start/Stop"; it will start the cooking process by building up inside pressure.
11. At the point when the clock goes off speedy discharge pressure by adjusting the pressure valve to "Vent".
12. After pressure gets released, open the pressure lid.

Glamorous Turkey Burger

PREPARATION
20 min

COOKING
21 min

SERVING
4

INGREDIENTS

- 1 large red onion, chopped
- ½ teaspoon pepper
- ¼ teaspoon salt
- 1 cup feta cheese, crumbled
- 2/3 cup sun-dried tomatoes, chopped
- 6 burger buns, sliced in half
- 2 lb. / 900g lean turkey, grounded
- 3 oz. / 85g plain granola

DIRECTIONS

1. Take a medium-sized mixing bowl and add listed ingredients
2. Combine them well and make 6 patties out of the mixture
3. Preheat your Ninja Foodi in "Med" mode setting the timer to 14 minutes
4. Wait till you hear the beep
5. Transfer the patties to your Ninja Foodi "Reversible Rack"
6. Cook for 7 minutes
7. Serve by placing them in your burger buns
8. Enjoy!

Daisy Fresh Maple Chicken

PREPARATION
10 min

COOKING
10 min

SERVING
4

INGREDIENTS

- 2 teaspoons onion powder
- 2 teaspoons garlic powder
- 3 garlic cloves, minced
- 1/3 cup soy sauce
- 1 cup maple syrup
- ¼ cup teriyaki sauce
- 1 teaspoon black pepper
- 2 lb. / 900g chicken wings, bone-in

DIRECTIONS

1. Take a medium-sized bowl and add soy sauce, garlic, pepper, maple syrup, garlic powder, onion powder, teriyaki sauce and mix well

2. Add the chicken wings to the mixture and coat it gently

3. Preheat your Ninja Foodi in "Med" mode, setting the timer to 10 minutes

4. Once you hear a beep, arrange your prepared wings in the grill grate

5. Cook for 5 minutes, fli and cook for 5 minutes more until the internal temperature reaches 165° F / 75° C

6. Serve!

The Tarragon Chicken Meal

PREPARATION
15 min

COOKING
4 min

SERVING
4

INGREDIENTS

For Chicken

- 1 ½ lb. / 680g chicken tenders
- Salt as needed
- 3 tablespoons tarragon leaves, chopped
- 1 teaspoon lemon zest, grated
- 2 tablespoons fresh lemon juice
- 2 tablespoons extra virgin olive oil

For Sauce

- 2 tablespoons fresh lemon juice
- 2 tablespoons butter, salted
- ½ cup heavy whip cream

DIRECTIONS

1. Prepare your chicken by taking a baking dish and arranging the chicken over the dish in a single layer
2. Season generously with salt and pepper
3. Sprinkle chopped tarragon and lemon zest all around the tenders
4. Drizzle lemon juice and olive oil on top
5. Let them sit for 10 minutes
6. Drain them well
7. Insert "Reversible Rack" in your Ninja Foodi and set to "High" temperature
8. Set timer to 4 minutes
9. Once you hear the beep, place chicken tenders in your "Reversible Rack"
10. Let it cook for 4 minutes until cooked completely
11. Do in batches if needed
12. Transfer the cooked chicken tenders to a platter
13. For the sauce, take a small-sized saucepan
14. Add cream, butter, and lemon juice and bring to a boil
15. Once thickened enough, pour the mix over chicken
16. Serve and enjoy once ready!

CHAPTER 9

Chicken And
Poultry Recipes

Popcorn Chicken

PREPARATION
20 min

COOKING
10 min

SERVING
2

INGREDIENTS

- 2 boneless, skinless chicken breasts
- 1 cup of breadcrumbs
- 2 beaten eggs
- 1 cup of flou
- 1 teaspoon of salt
- 1 teaspoon of black pepper
- 1 teaspoon of onion powder
- 1 teaspoon of garlic powder

DIRECTIONS

1. Select "Air Fry" to 390° F / 200° C and preheat.
2. Using a food processor, add the chicken breasts and beat it until it minced properly.
3. Using two bowls, add the flour the eggs and mix it properly into the firs bowl, then in the second bowl, add the breadcrumbs, seasonings and mix it properly.
4. Mold the minced chicken into small balls.
5. Cover the minced chicken in the flour dip it into the egg wash, and then cover it with the seasoned breadcrumbs.
6. Place it inside your Ninja Foodi ("Air Fry" mode) and cook it for 10 minutes at 390° F / 200° C or until it is fully done.
7. Serve and enjoy!

Honey Teriyaki Chicken

PREPARATION
6 min

COOKING
30 min

SERVING
4

INGREDIENTS

- 4 chicken breasts, sliced into strips
- 1 cup of soy sauce
- 1/2 cup water
- 2/3 cup honey
- 2 teaspoons garlic, minced
- 1/2 cup rice vinegar
- 1/2 teaspoon ground ginger
- 1/4 teaspoon crushed red pepper flake
- 3 tablespoons cornstarch dissolved in 3 tablespoons cold water

DIRECTIONS

1. Put the chicken inside the Ninja Foodi.
2. Add the rest of the ingredients except the corn starch mixture.
3. Put on the lid. Set it to pressure, cook at "High" pressure for 30 minutes.
4. Release the pressure naturally. Set it to "Sauté".
5. Stir in the cornstarch and simmer until the sauce has thickened.

Serving Suggestion:

Garnish with sesame seeds and serve with fried rice.

Tips:

Use low sodium soy sauce.

Grilled Chicken Tacos

PREPARATION
14 min

COOKING
18 min

SERVING
8

INGREDIENTS

- 2 tablespoons chipotle in adobo sauce, chopped
- 2 teaspoons sugar
- 1/3 cup olive oil
- 1/3 cup lime juice
- 1/3 cup red wine vinegar
- 2 teaspoons salt 2
- teaspoons pepper
- 1 cup fresh cilantro, chopped
- 2 lbs. / 900g boneless skinless chicken thighs
- Taco wraps: 8 flou tortillas
- 4 poblano peppers 1
- tablespoon olive oil
- 2 cups shredded Jack cheese

DIRECTIONS

1. Take the firs six ingredients in a blender jug and blend them.
2. Once blended, mix with chipotles and cilantro.
3. Mix chicken with this cilantro marinade and cover to refrigerate for 8 hours.
4. Grease the poblanos with cooking oil and keep them aside.
5. Prepare and preheat the Ninja Foodi on a "High" setting.
6. Once it is preheated, open the lid and place the peppers in the grill.
7. Cover the Ninja Foodi's lid and let it grill on the "Grill" mode for 2 minutes.
8. Flip the peppers and then continue grilling for another 2 minutes.
9. It's time to grill the chicken in the same grill.
10. Place the chicken in the grill and cover the lid.
11. Select the "High" setting.
12. Grill the chicken for 5 minutes per side then transfer to a plate.
13. Now peel and slice the peppers in half then also slice the chicken.
14. Spread each tortilla and add half cup chicken, half peppers, and ¼ cup cheese.
15. Fold the tortilla and carefully place in the grill and cover its lid.
16. Grill each for 2 minutes per side on the "Med" temperature setting. Serve.

Turkey Burrito

PREPARATION
10 min

COOKING
8 min

SERVING
2

INGREDIENTS

- 4 slices turkey breast already cooked
- ½ red bell pepper, sliced
- 2 eggs
- 1 small avocado, peeled, pitted, and sliced
- 2 tablespoons salsa
- Salt and black pepper to the taste
- 1/8 cup mozzarella cheese, grated
- Tortillas for serving

DIRECTIONS

1. In a bowl, whisk eggs with salt and pepper to the taste, pour them in a pan and place it in the Ninja Foodi's Cook & Crisp basket.

2. Cook at 400° F / 205° C for 5 minutes, take the pan out of the Ninja, and transfer eggs to a plate.

3. Roll your burritos and place them in your Ninja Foodi after you've lined it with some tin foil.

4. Heat the burritos at 300° F / 150° C for 3 minutes, divide them among plates and serve.

5. Enjoy!

Honey & Rosemary Chicken

PREPARATION
15 min

COOKING
35 min

SERVING
6

INGREDIENTS

- 1 teaspoon paprika
- Salt to taste
- 1/2 teaspoon baking powder
- 2 lb. / 900g chicken wings
- 1/4 cup honey
- 1 tablespoon lemon juice
- 1 tablespoon garlic, minced
- 1 tablespoon rosemary, chopped

DIRECTIONS

1. Choose a "Air Fry" setting in your Ninja Foodi.
2. Set it to 390 F / 200° C.
3. Set the time to 30 minutes.
4. Press start to preheat.
5. While waiting, mix the paprika, salt, and baking powder in a bowl.
6. Add the wings to the Cook & Crisp basket.
7. Close and cook for 15 minutes.
8. Flip and cook for another 15 minutes.
9. In a bowl, mix the remaining ingredients.
10. Coat the wings with the sauce and cook for another 5 minutes.

Serving Suggestions:

Serve with the remaining sauce.

Tips:

You can also add crushed red peeper to the spice mixture.

Mustard Chicken

PREPARATION
10 min

COOKING
45 min

SERVING
4

INGREDIENTS

- 1/4 cup Dijon mustard
- 1/4 cup cooking oil
- Salt and pepper to taste
- 2 tablespoons honey
- 1 tablespoon dry oregano
- 2 teaspoons dry Italian seasoning
- 1 tablespoon lemon juice
- 6 chicken pieces

DIRECTIONS

1. Combine all the ingredients except chicken in a bowl.
2. Mix well.
3. Toss the chicken in the mixture.
4. Add Reversible rack to your Ninja Foodi.
5. Choose "Roast" function.
6. Set it to 350° F / 180° C.
7. Cook for 25 minutes.
8. Flip and cook for another 20 minutes.

Serving Suggestions:

Serve with hot sauce.

Tips:

Use freshly squeezed lemon juice.

Grilled Chicken with Veggies

PREPARATION
20 min

COOKING
25 min

SERVING
2

INGREDIENTS

- 2 chicken thighs and legs
- 2 tablespoons oil, divided
- Salt and pepper to taste
- 1 onion, diced
- 1/4 cup mushrooms, sliced
- 1 cup potatoes, diced
- 1 tablespoon lemon juice
- 1 tablespoon honey
- 4 sprigs fresh thyme, chopped
- 2 cloves garlic, crushed and minced

DIRECTIONS

1. Add the Grill grate to your Ninja Foodi.
2. Put the veggie tray on top of the Grill grate.
3. Close the hood.
4. Choose the "Grill" function and set it to "High".
5. Press "Start" to preheat.
6. Brush the chicken with half of the oil.
7. Season with salt and pepper.
8. Toss the onion, mushrooms, and potatoes in the remaining oil.
9. Sprinkle it with salt and pepper.
10. Add chicken to the grill grate.
11. Add the potato mixture to the veggie tray.
12. Close the hood and cook for 15 minutes.
13. Flip chicken and toss potatoes.
14. Cook for another 10 minutes.

Serving Suggestions:

Serve chicken with the veggies on the side. Garnish with herb sprigs.

Tips:

Add more cooking time if you want skin crispier.

Grilled Garlic Chicken

PREPARATION
5 min

COOKING
15 min

SERVING
8

INGREDIENTS

- 3 lb. / 1.4 kg chicken thigh fillet
- Garlic salt to taste

DIRECTIONS

1. Add Grill plate to the Ninja Foodi.
2. Preheat to "Med" heat.
3. Sprinkle chicken with garlic salt on both sides.
4. Select "Grill" and cook for 8 minutes.
5. Flip and cook for another 7 minutes.

Serving Suggestions:

Serve with hot sauce and mustard. Serve with fries on the side.

Tips:

Add cooking time to make the skin crispier.

Honey-Mustard Chicken Tenders

PREPARATION
5 min

COOKING
4 min

SERVING
4

INGREDIENTS

- ½ cup Dijon mustard
- 2 tablespoons honey
- 2 tablespoons olive oil
- 1 teaspoon freshly ground black pepper
- 2 lb. / 900g chicken tenders
- ½ cup walnuts

DIRECTIONS

1. Whisk together the mustard, honey, olive oil, and pepper in a medium bowl. Add the chicken and toss to coat.

2. Finely grind the walnuts by pulsing them in a food processor or putting them in a heavy-duty plastic bag and pounding them with a rolling pin or heavy skillet.

3. Insert the Grill Grate and close the hood. Select "Grill", set the temperature to "High", and set the timer to 4 minutes. Select "Start/ Stop" to begin preheating.

4. Toss the chicken tenders in the ground walnuts to coat them lightly.

5. Grill the chicken tenders for 4 minutes, until they have taken on grill marks and are cooked through. Serve hot, at room temperature, or refrigerate and serve cold.

Rosemary Chicken

PREPARATION
5 min

COOKING
6 min

SERVING
4

INGREDIENTS

- ½ cup balsamic vinegar
- 2 tablespoons olive oil
- 2 rosemary sprigs, coarsely chopped
- 2 lb. / 900g boneless, skinless chicken breasts, pounded to a ½ inch / 1.3 cm thickness

DIRECTIONS

1. Combine the balsamic vinegar, olive oil, and rosemary in a shallow baking dish. Add the chicken breasts and turn to coat. Cover with plastic wrap and refrigerate for at least 30 minutes or overnight.

2. Insert the Grill Grate and close the hood. Select "Grill", set the temperature to "High", and set the timer to 6 minutes. Select "Start/Stop" to begin preheating.

3. When the unit beeps to signify it has preheated, place the s chicken breasts on the Grill Grate. Close the hood and cook for 6 minutes until they have taken on grill marks and are cooked through.

Grilled Balsamic Chicken Breast

PREPARATION
10 min

COOKING
20 min

SERVING
4

INGREDIENTS

- 1/4 cup olive oil
- 2 tablespoons balsamic vinegar
- 3 teaspoon garlic, minced
- 3 tablespoons soy sauce
- 1 tablespoon Worcestershire sauce
- 1/4 cup brown sugar
- Salt and pepper to taste
- 4 chicken breast fillets

DIRECTIONS

1. In a bowl, mix all ingredients except chicken.
2. Reserve 1/4 cup of the mixture for later.
3. Marinate the chicken breast in the remaining mixture for 30 minutes.
4. Add Grill grate to the Ninja Foodi.
5. Set it to "Grill" for 20 minutes.
6. Add the chicken breast and close the hood.
7. Cook for 10 minutes.
8. Flip and cook for another 5 minutes.
9. Baste with remaining sauce. Cook for 5 more minutes.
10. Serve with remaining sauce if any.

Serving Suggestions:

Let the chicken rest for 5 minutes before serving.

Tips:

For thick chicken breast fillets, flatte   with a meat mallet.

Barbecue Chicken Breast

PREPARATION
10 min

COOKING
30 min

SERVING
4

INGREDIENTS

- 4 chicken breast fillets
- 2 tablespoons vegetable oil
- Salt and pepper to taste
- 1 cup barbecue sauce

DIRECTIONS

1. Add Grill grate to the Ninja Foodi.
2. Close the hood.
3. Choose a "Grill" setting.
4. Preheat to medium for 30 minutes.
5. Press "Start".
6. Brush chicken breast with oil.
7. Sprinkle both sides with salt and pepper.
8. Add chicken and cook for 10 minutes.
9. Flip and cook for another 10 minutes.
10. Brush chicken with barbecue sauce.
11. Cook for 5 minutes.
12. Brush the other side and cook for another 5 minutes.

Serving Suggestions:

Serve with mashed potato and gravy.

Tips:

You can also use homemade barbecue sauce simply by mixing ketchup, sugar, minced garlic, lemon juice, and soy sauce.

CHAPTER 10

Easy Fish and Seafood Recipes

Shrimp Fajitas

PREPARATION
20 min

COOKING
20 min

SERVING
12

INGREDIENTS

- 1 lb. / 450g shrimp, peeled and deveined
- 1 onion, diced
- 2 tablespoons taco seasoning
- Cooking spray
- Tortillas

DIRECTIONS

1. Spray Cook & Crisp basket with oil.
2. Mix shrimp, onion, and bell peppers in a bowl.
3. Spray with oil and season with taco seasoning.
4. Set your Ninja Foodi to "Air Fry".
5. Add shrimp mixture to the basket.
6. Air fry at 390° F / 200° C for 10 minutes.
7. Shake and cook for another 10 minutes.
8. Spread on top of tortillas.

Serving Suggestions:

Serve with hot sauce.

Spiced Up Grilled Shrimp

PREPARATION
5-10 min

COOKING
6 min

SERVING
4

INGREDIENTS

- 2 tablespoons brown sugar
- 1 lb. / 450g jumbo shrimp, peeled and deveined
- 2 tablespoons olive oil
- 1 tablespoon garlic powder
- 1 tablespoon paprika
- ½ teaspoon black pepper
- 1 teaspoon garlic salt

DIRECTIONS

1. Take a bowl and add listed ingredients gently mix
2. Let the mixture chill for 30-60 minutes
3. Preheat in "Grill" mode "Med" and set timer to 6 minutes
4. Once you hear the beep, arrange your prepared shrimp over the grill grate
5. Lock and let it cook for 3 minutes
6. Flip and cook for 3 minutes more
7. Once done, serve and enjoy!

Tuna Patties

PREPARATION
Average **12** min

COOKING
10 min

SERVING
4

INGREDIENTS

- 2 cans tuna flake
- 1/2 tablespoon almond flou
- 1 teaspoon dried dill
- 1 tablespoon mayo
- 1/2 teaspoon onion powder
- 1 teaspoon garlic powder
- Salt and pepper to taste
- 1 tablespoon lemon juice

DIRECTIONS

1. Mix all the ingredients in a bowl.
2. Form patties.
3. Set the tuna patties on the Ninja Foodi basket
4. Seal the crisping lid.
5. Set it to "Air Fry".
6. Cook at 400° F / 205° C for 5 minutes.
7. Flip and cook for 5 more minutes.

Serving Suggestion: Serve with a fresh green salad.

Lemon Garlic Shrimp

PREPARATION
10 min

COOKING
10 min

SERVING
4

INGREDIENTS

- 1 lb. / 450g shrimp, peeled and deveined
- 1 tablespoon olive oil
- 4 cloves garlic, minced
- 1 tablespoon lemon juice
- Salt to taste

DIRECTIONS

1. Mix the olive oil, salt, lemon juice, and garlic. Toss shrimp in the mixture.
2. Marinate for 15 minutes.
3. Place the shrimp in the Ninja Foodi basket.
4. Seal the crisping lid. Select the "Air Fry" setting.
5. Cook at 350° F / 180° C for 7 minutes.
6. Flip and cook for 3 more minutes.

Serving Suggestion:

Sprinkle chopped parsley on top.

Honey Garlic Shrimp

PREPARATION
15 min

COOKING
25 min

SERVING
6

INGREDIENTS

- 1/2 cup tamari
- 1/2 cup honey
- 1 clove garlic, crushed
- 1 teaspoon fresh ginger
- 2 tablespoons ketchup
- 2 tablespoons cornstarch
- 16 oz. / 450g shrimp, peeled and deveined
- 16 oz. / 450g frozen vegetables

DIRECTIONS

1. Add tamari, honey, garlic, ginger, and ketchup in a pan over "Med" heat.
2. "Slow Cook" mode for 10 minutes.
3. Stir in cornstarch and "Slow Cook" for 5 minutes.
4. Dip shrimp in the sauce.
5. Add shrimp to the Cook & Crisp basket.
6. Set your Ninja Foodi to "Air Fry".
7. Air fry at 355° F / 180° C for 10 minutes.

Serving Suggestions:
Serve with hot brown rice.

Tips:
You can also use pre-peeled shrimp to save time.

Lovely Crab Soup

PREPARATION
5 min

COOKING
around **180** min

SERVING
4

INGREDIENTS

- 1 cup crab meat, cubed
- 1 tablespoon garlic, minced
- Salt as needed
- Red chili flake as needed
- 3 cups vegetable broth
- 1 teaspoon salt

DIRECTIONS

1. Coat the crab cubes in lime juice and let them sit for a while
2. Add the all ingredients (including marinated crab meat) to your Ninja Foodi and lock the lid
3. Cook on "Slow Cook" mode ("Med") for 3 hours
4. Let it sit for a while
5. Unlock lid and set to "Sauté" mode, simmer the soup for 5 minutes more on "Low"
6. Stir and check to season. Enjoy!

Crumbed Flounder Fillet

PREPARATION
10 min

COOKING
12 min

SERVING
4

INGREDIENTS

- ¼ cup vegetable oil
- 1 cup breadcrumbs
- 4 flounde fillets
- 1 egg, beaten

DIRECTIONS

1. Set Ninja Foodi to "Air Fry".
2. Preheat to 350° F / 180° C.
3. Combine oil and breadcrumbs in a bowl.
4. Mix until crumbly.
5. Coat the fis with egg and dredge with the breadcrumb mixture.
6. Add fis fillet to the Cook & Crisp basket.
7. Cook for 12 minutes.

Serving Suggestions:

Garnish with lemon wedges.

Tips:

You can also use olive oil in place of vegetable oil.

Teriyaki Coho Glazed Salmon

PREPARATION
10 min

COOKING
25 min

SERVING
4

INGREDIENTS

- 1-2 coho salmon filet
- 1 cup of water
- ¼ cup of soy sauce
- ¼ cup brown sugar
- 1 tablespoon honey
- 1 ½ tablespoons ginger roots, minced
- ½ teaspoon white pepper
- 2 tablespoons cornstarch
- ¼ cup of cold water

DIRECTIONS

1. Insert the Grill grate and close the hood
2. Preheat Ninja Foodi by pressing the "Grill" option and setting it to "High" for 15 minutes
3. Take a medium saucepan over medium heat, combine sauce ingredients (except salmon, cornstarch, and cold water) and bring to a low boil
4. Then add cornstarch and water in another bowl, whisk cornstarch mixture slowly into sauce until it thickens
5. Add one chunk of pecan wood to the hot coal of your grill
6. Brush sauce onto the salmon file
7. Place on the grill grate, then close the hood
8. Cook for 15 minutes
9. Brush the salmon with another coat of sauce
10. Close the lid and cook for 10 minutes more
11. Serve and enjoy!

Adventurous Sweet and Sour Fish

PREPARATION
10 min

COOKING
6 min

SERVING
4

INGREDIENTS

- 2 drops liquid stevia
- 1/4 cup butter
- 1 lb. / 450g fis   chunks
- 1 tablespoon vinegar
- Salt and pepper to taste

DIRECTIONS

1. Set your Ninja Foodi to "Sauté" mode and add butter, let it melt

2. Add fis   chunks and Sauté for 3 minutes. Add stevia, salt, and pepper, stir

3. Lock Crisping Lid and cook on "Air Fry" mode for 3 minutes at 360° F / 180° C

4. Serve once done and enjoy it!

Garlic and Lemon Prawn Delight

PREPARATION
5 min

COOKING
5 min

SERVING
4

INGREDIENTS

- 2 tablespoons olive oil
- 1 lb. / 450g prawns
- 2 tablespoons garlic, minced
- 2/3 cup fis stock
- 1 tablespoon butter
- 2 tablespoons lemon juice
- 1 tablespoon lemon zest
- Salt and pepper to taste

DIRECTIONS

1. Set your Ninja Foodi to "Sauté" mode and add butter and oil, let it heat up

2. Stir in remaining ingredients. Lock lid and cook on "Low" pressure for 5 minutes

3. Quick-release pressure. Serve and enjoy!

Crispy Fish Sandwich

PREPARATION
15 min

COOKING
12 min

SERVING
2

INGREDIENTS

Tartar Sauce

- 1/4 cup mayonnaise
- 1 teaspoon pickle juice
- 2 tablespoons dill pickles, chopped

Fish Sandwiches

- 2 white fis   fillet
- 2 teaspoons Old Bay Seasoning
- 2 tablespoons flou
- 1 egg, beaten
- 1/2 cup breadcrumbs
- 2 slices low-fat cheese slices
- 2 burger buns

DIRECTIONS

1. Mix mayo, pickle juice, and dill pickles in a bowl.
2. Cover and place inside the refrigerator.
3. Add seasoning and flour in a dish.
4. Beat egg in a bowl.
5. Put breadcrumbs in the third bowl.
6. Coat fish fillets with flour mixture.
7. Dip in egg and then dredge with breadcrumbs.
8. Add fish fillets to the Cook & Crisp basket.
9. Set Ninja Foodi to "Air Fry".
10. Cook at 350° F / 180° C for 12 minutes.
11. Add crispy fish to burger buns.
12. Top with tartar sauce and cheese.

Serving Suggestions:

Serve with cucumber and tomato salad.

Crispy Fish Nuggets

PREPARATION
10 min

COOKING
15 min

SERVING
4

INGREDIENTS

- 1 lb. / 450g cod fillet sliced into 8 pieces
- Salt and pepper to taste
- 1/2 cup flou
- 1 tablespoon egg with 1 teaspoon water
- 1 cup bread crumbs
- 1 tablespoon vegetable oil

DIRECTIONS

1. Season the fis with salt and pepper. Cover with the flour

2. Dip the fis in the egg wash and into the bread crumbs.

3. Place the fis nuggets in the Ninja Foodi Cook & Crisp basket. Set it to "Air Fry" function.

4. Seal with the crisping lid. Cook at 360° F / 180° C for 15 minutes.

Serving Suggestion:

Serve with lemon honey tartar sauce.

Packets of Lemon And Dill Cod

PREPARATION
10 min

COOKING
5 min

SERVING
4

INGREDIENTS

- 2 tilapia cod fillets
- Salt, pepper, and garlic powder to taste
- 2 sprigs fresh dill
- 4 slices lemon
- 2 tablespoons butter

DIRECTIONS

1. Layout 2 large squares of parchment paper
2. Place fille in the center of each parchment square and season with salt, pepper, and garlic powder
3. On each fillet place 1 sprig of dill, 2 lemon slices, 1 tablespoon butter
4. Place trivet at the bottom of your Ninja Foodi. Add 1 cup water into the pot
5. Close parchment paper around fillet and fold to make a nice seal
6. Place both packets in your pot. Lock lid and cook on "High" pressure for 5 minutes
7. Quick-release pressure. Serve and enjoy!

Grilled Paprika Salmon

PREPARATION
10 min

COOKING
10 min

SERVING
2

INGREDIENTS

- 2 salmon fillets
- Pinch paprika
- Salt and pepper to taste

DIRECTIONS

1. Insert Grill grate to the Ninja Foodi.
2. Choose the "Grill" function.
3. Set it to "High" and preheat for 10 minutes.
4. Season salmon with paprika, salt, and pepper.
5. Add salmon to the grill.
6. Cook for 5 minutes per side.

Serving Suggestions:

Serve with pasta salad.

Salmon Paprika

PREPARATION
5 min

COOKING
7 min

SERVING
4

INGREDIENTS

- 2 wild-caught salmon fillets 1 ½ inch / 3.8 cm thick
- 2 teaspoons paprika
- 2 teaspoons avocado oil
- Green herbs, to garnish
- Salt and pepper to taste

DIRECTIONS

1. Season salmon fillet with salt, pepper, paprika, and olive oil
2. Place Cook & Crisp basket in your Ninja Foodi
3. Select "Pressure" and preheat your Ninja Foodie at 390° F / 200° C
4. Place seasoned fillet inside Ninja Foodie
5. Seal the Crisping lid and cook for 7 minutes
6. Add herbs on top
7. Serve and enjoy!

Fish Tacos

PREPARATION
10 min

COOKING
11 min

SERVING
4

INGREDIENTS

- 4 cod fillets cut into 1 inch / 2.5 cm cubes
- Salt and black pepper to taste
- ½ lime, juiced
- ½ cup all-purpose flou
- 1 large egg, lightly beaten
- 1 cup panko breadcrumbs
- Olive oil for brushing
- 4 medium corn tortillas
- ½ cup shredded red cabbage
- 1 medium avocado, pitted, peeled, and chopped
- 2 tbsp. chopped fresh cilantro
- 1 cup sour cream
- Lime wedges for serving

DIRECTIONS

1. Insert the Crisper pan in the bottom part of the air fryer and preheat on "Air Fry" mode at 400° F / 205° C for 2 to 3 minutes. Lightly brush the rotisserie basket with some olive oil and set aside.

2. Season the fis with salt, black pepper, and lime juice.

3. Pour the flou onto a plate and the breadcrumbs onto another. Dredge the fis pieces lightly on the flour then in the eggs and the breadcrumbs. Put the coated fis in the Cook & Crisp basket.

4. Set the timer for 9 minutes or until the fis pieces are golden brown.

5. To serve, lay the tortillas individually on a clean, fla surface and add the fis pieces. Top with the cabbage, avocado, cilantro, sour cream, and lime wedges.

6. Serve immediately.

Crispy Cod Fish

PREPARATION
10 min

COOKING
5 min

SERVING
4

INGREDIENTS

- 4 cod fis   fillet
- Salt and sugar to taste
- 1 teaspoon sesame oil
- 8 fl. oz. / 250 ml water
- 5 tablespoons light soy sauce
- 1 teaspoon dark soy sauce
- 3 tablespoons oil
- 5 slices ginger

DIRECTIONS

1. Pat the codfis   fillet dry.
2. Season with the salt, sugar, and sesame oil. Marinate for 15 minutes.
3. Set the Ninja Foodi to "Air Fry".
4. Put the fis   on top of the basket. Cook at 350° F / 180° C for 3 minutes.
5. Flip and cook for 2 minutes. Take the fis   out and set aside.
6. Put the rest of the ingredients in the pot.
7. Set it to "Sauté". Simmer and pour over the fis   before serving.

Serving Suggestion:

Sprinkle top with chopped green onion.

Zesty Ranch Fish Fillets

PREPARATION
10 min

COOKING
15 min

SERVING
4

INGREDIENTS

- ¾ cup finely crushed cornflake or panko breadcrumbs
- 3 tbsp. dry ranch-style dressing mix
- 1 tsp. fresh lemon zest
- 2 ½ tbsp. olive oil
- 2 eggs, beaten
- 4 white fish fillets
- Lemon wedges to garnish

DIRECTIONS

1. Insert the Crisper pan in the bottom part of the Ninja Foodi and preheat on "Air Fry" mode at 400° F / 205° C for 2 to 3 minutes.
2. Mix the cornflakes dressing mix, lemon zest, and oil on a shallow plate and then pour the eggs on another.
3. Working in two batches, dip the fis into the egg, drip off excess egg, and coat well in the cornflake' mixture on both sides.
4. Place the fis   on the Deluxe Reversible Rack and fi   the tray on the middle rack of the oven. Close the oven and set the timer for 13 minutes and cook until the fis   is golden brown and the fis   flak   within.
5. Transfer to a serving plate and serve with the lemon wedges.

Salmon with Coconut Aminos

PREPARATION
15 min

COOKING
15 min

SERVING
4

INGREDIENTS

- 1/2 teaspoon ginger powder
- 1/2 teaspoon garlic powder
- 1 tablespoon honey
- 4 tablespoons Coconut Aminos
- Salt and pepper to taste
- 3 salmon fillets

DIRECTIONS

1. Mix ginger powder, garlic powder, honey, Coconut Aminos, salt, and pepper in a bowl.
2. Coat the salmon fillets with this mixture.
3. Marinate for 30 minutes, covered in the refrigerator.
4. Add fish to the Cook & Crisp basket.
5. Set your Ninja Foodi to "Air Fry".
6. Cook at 390° F / 200° C for 15 minutes.

Serving Suggestions:

Garnish with lemon slices.

Tips:

Do not overcrowd the Cook & Crisp basket to ensure even cooking. Cook in batches if necessary.

Beer-Battered Cod

PREPARATION
15 min

COOKING
15 min

SERVING
4

INGREDIENTS

- 1 cup all-purpose flou
- ½ teaspoon baking soda
- 2 tablespoons cornstarch
- 1 egg, beaten
- 6 fl. oz. / 170 ml beer
- 4 cod fillet
- ½ teaspoon paprika
- Pinch cayenne pepper
- Salt and pepper to taste
- Vegetable oil

DIRECTIONS

1. Mix flour baking soda, cornstarch, egg, and beer in a bowl.
2. Sprinkle cod fillet with paprika, cayenne, salt, and pepper.
3. Dip in the flou mixture.
4. Drizzle with oil.
5. Add to the Cook & Crisp basket.
6. Choose "Air Fry" setting in your Ninja Foodi.
7. Cook at 390° F / 200° C for 12 to 15 minutes.

Serving Suggestions:

Serve with coleslaw.

Tips:

Refrigerate flou mixture for 20 minutes before using it.

Authentic Garlic Salmon Meal

PREPARATION
10 min

COOKING
6 min

SERVING
3

INGREDIENTS

- 2 salmon fillet 6 oz. / 170g each
- 1 garlic cloves, minced
- ¼ teaspoon salt
- ¼ teaspoon fresh rosemary, minced
- 1 teaspoon lemon zest, grated
- ¼ teaspoon pepper

DIRECTIONS

1. Take a bowl and add listed ingredients except for your salmon. Mix the whole mixture well

2. Add salmon to the mix and let the fis sit in the marinade for 15 minutes

3. Preheat your Ninja Foodi in "Sauté" mode at "Med" with the timer set to 6 minutes

4. Once you hear the beep, transfer prepared salmon over the Reversible Rack grate

5. Cook for 3 minutes, fli and cook for 3 minutes more

6. Serve and enjoy once ready!

Grilled Shrimp

PREPARATION
10 min

COOKING
8 min

SERVING
8

INGREDIENTS

- 2 lb. / 900g shrimp, deveined
- 2 tablespoons olive oil
- 1 tablespoon Old Bay Seasoning
- Garlic salt to taste

DIRECTIONS

1. Set "Grill" mode at "Med" and preheat.
2. Brush shrimp with olive oil.
3. Season with Old Bay seasoning and garlic salt.
4. Cook for 4 minutes per side.

Serving Suggestions:

Serve with grilled corn.

Tips:

Add cayenne pepper if you want your shrimp spicier.

Shrimp Boil

PREPARATION
8 min

COOKING
13 min

SERVING
6

INGREDIENTS

- 12 oz. / 340g shrimp, peeled and deveined
- 14 oz. / 400g smoked sausage, sliced
- 4 corn on cobs, sliced into 4
- 3 cups potatoes, sliced in half and boiled
- 1/8 cup Old Bay seasoning
- 1/4 cup white onion, diced
- Cooking spray

DIRECTIONS

1. Mix all the ingredients in the inner pot of the Ninja Foodi.
2. Spray mixture with oil.
3. Set the unit to "Air Fry".
4. Air fry at 390° F / 200° C for 7 minutes.
5. Stir and cook for another 6 minutes.

Serving Suggestions:

Sprinkle with dried herbs before serving.

Tips:

Check the dish halfway through cooking to see if it's cooking evenly.

Swordfish with Caper Sauce

PREPARATION
10 min

COOKING
10 min

SERVING
4

INGREDIENTS

- Pepper as needed
- Salt as needed
- 2 tablespoon capers drained
- 1 tablespoon extra-virgin olive oil
- 1 tablespoon lemon juice
- 1 lemon, sliced into 8 slices
- 4 tablespoons unsalted butter
- 4 swordfis steaks, 1 inch / 2.5 cm thick

DIRECTIONS

1. Take a large shallow bowl and whisk together the lemon juice and oil
2. Season with swordfish steaks with salt and pepper on each side, place in the oil mixture
3. Turn to coat both sides and refrigerate for 15 minutes
4. Insert the Grill grate and close the hood
5. Preheat Ninja Foodi by pressing the "Grill" option at and setting it to "Max" and timer to 9 minutes
6. Let it preheat until you hear a beep
7. Arrange the swordfish over the grill grate, lock lid, and cook for 9 minutes
8. Place a medium saucepan over "Med" heat and melt butter
9. Add the lemon slices and capers to the pan and cook for 1 minute
10. Then turn off the heat
11. Remove the swordfish from the grill and serve with caper sauce over it
12. Enjoy!

Home Haddock

PREPARATION
5-10 min

COOKING
13 min

SERVING
3

INGREDIENTS

- ¼ teaspoon salt
- ¾ cup breadcrumbs
- ¼ cup parmesan cheese, grated
- ¼ teaspoon ground thyme
- ¼ cup butter, melted
- 1 lb. / 450g haddock fillet
- ¾ cup milk

DIRECTIONS

1. Take the fis fillet and carefully dredge them in milk
2. Season them well with salt, keep them on the side
3. Take a medium-sized bowl, add cheese, thyme, parmesan, breadcrumbs, and mix
4. Take your fillet and coat them with breadcrumbs
5. Preheat your Ninja Foodi in "Bake" mode to a temperature of 325° F / 160° C, setting the timer to 13 minutes
6. Once you hear the beep, the appliance is ready
7. Transfer the prepared fillet to Reversible Rack and cook for 8 minutes, fli and cook for 5 minutes more
8. Once you have a flak texture, serve, and enjoy!

Awesome Magical 5 Ingredient Shrimp

PREPARATION
10 min

COOKING
15 min

SERVING
4

INGREDIENTS

- 2 tablespoons butter
- 1/2 teaspoon smoked paprika
- 1 lb. / 450g shrimps, peeled and deveined
- Lemongrass stalks
- 1 red chili pepper, seeded and chopped

DIRECTIONS

1. Take a bowl and mix all of the ingredients well, except lemongrass and marinate for 1 hour
2. Transfer to Ninja Foodi and lock lid, "Bake/Roast" for 15 minutes at 350° F / 180° C
3. Once done, serve and enjoy!

Fish Sticks

PREPARATION
15 min

COOKING
15 min

SERVING
8

INGREDIENTS

- 16 oz. / 450g tilapia fillets sliced into strips
- 1 cup all-purpose flou
- 2 eggs
- 1 1/2 cups breadcrumbs
- Salt to taste

DIRECTIONS

1. Dip fis   strips in flou and then in eggs.
2. Mix breadcrumbs and salt.
3. Coat fis   strips with breadcrumbs.
4. Add fis   strips to the Cook & Crisp basket.
5. Place the Cook & Crisp basket inside the Ninja Foodi.
6. Choose "Air Fry" setting.
7. Cook fis   strips at 390° F / 200° C for 12 to 15 minutes, flippin   once halfway through.

Serving Suggestions:

Serve with tartar sauce and ketchup.

CHAPTER 11

Easy Beef and Lamb Recipes

Quick Picadillo Dish

PREPARATION
10 min

COOKING
16 min

SERVING
4

INGREDIENTS

- 1/2 lb. / 225g lean ground beef
- 2 garlic cloves, minced
- 1/2 large onion, chopped
- 1 teaspoon salt
- 1 tomato, chopped
- 1/2 red bell pepper, chopped
- 1 tablespoon cilantro
- 1/2 can (4 oz. / 115g) tomato sauce
- 1 teaspoon ground cumin
- 1-2 bay leaves
- 2 tablespoons green olives, capers
- 2 tablespoons brine
- 3 tablespoons water

DIRECTIONS

1. Set your Ninja Foodi to "Sauté" mode and add meat, salt, and pepper, slightly brown

2. Add garlic, tomato, onion, cilantro, and Sauté for 1 minute. Add olives, brine, leaf, cumin, and mix

3. Pour in sauce, water, and stir. Lock lid and cook on "High" pressure for 15 minutes

4. Quick-release pressure

Lettuce Cheese Steak

PREPARATION
10 min

COOKING
12 min

SERVING
5-6

INGREDIENTS

- 4 (8 oz. / 225g) skirt steaks
- 6 cups romaine lettuce, chopped
- ¾ cup cherry tomatoes halved
- ¼ cup blue cheese, crumbled
- Ocean salt and Ground Black Pepper
- 2 avocados, peeled and sliced
- 1 cup croutons
- 1 cup blue cheese dressing

DIRECTIONS

1. Coat steaks with black pepper and salt.
2. Take Ninja Foodi, mastermind it over your kitchen stage, and open the top. Organize the barbecue mesh and close the top.
3. Click "Grill" and choose the "High" function. Change the clock to 8 minutes and afterward press "Start/Stop." Ninja Foodi will begin pre-warming.
4. Ninja Foodi is preheated and prepared to cook when it begins to blare. After you hear a blare, open the top cover.
5. Fix finel the 2 steaks on the barbeque mesh.
6. Close the top cover and cook for 4 minutes. Presently open the top cover, fli the steaks.
7. Close the top cover and cook for 4 additional minutes. Cook until the food thermometer comes to 165° F / 75° C. Cook for 3-4 more minutes if needed. Grill the remaining steaks.
8. In a mixing bowl, add the lettuce, tomatoes, blue cheese, and croutons. Combine the ingredients to mix well with each other.
9. Serve the steaks warm with the salad mixture, blue cheese dressing, and avocado slices on top.

Grilled Beef Burgers

PREPARATION
20 min

COOKING
around **11** min

SERVING
4

INGREDIENTS

- 4 oz. / 115g cream cheese
- 4 slices bacon, cooked and crumbled
- 2 seeded jalapeño peppers, stemmed, and minced
- ½ cup shredded Cheddar cheese
- ½ teaspoon chili powder
- ¼ teaspoon paprika
- ¼ teaspoon ground black pepper
- 2 lb. / 900g ground beef
- 4 hamburger buns
- 4 slices pepper Jack cheese
- Optional - Lettuce, sliced tomato, and sliced red onion

DIRECTIONS

1. In a mixing bowl, combine the peppers, Cheddar cheese, cream cheese, and bacon until well combined.
2. Prepare the ground beef into 8 patties. Add the cheese mixture onto four of the patties; arrange a second patty on top of each to prepare four burgers. Press gently.
3. In another bowl, combine the chili powder, paprika, and pepper. Sprinkle the mixture onto the sides of the burgers.
4. Take Ninja Foodi, organize it over your kitchen stage, and open the top cover.
5. Organize the flam broil mesh and close the top cover.
6. Press "Broil" and select the "High" barbecue work. Change the clock to 4 minutes and afterward press "Start/Stop". Ninja Foodi will begin pre-warming.
7. Ninja Foodi is preheated and prepared to cook when it begins to blare. After you hear a blare, open the top. Arrange the burgers over the Reversible Rack.
8. Close the top lid and allow it to cook until the timer reads zero. Cook for 3-4 more minutes, if needed.
9. Cook until the food thermometer reaches 145° F / 65° C. Serve warm.
10. Serve warm with buns. Add your choice of toppings: pepper Jack cheese, lettuce, tomato, and red onion.

Beef Stew

PREPARATION
10 min

COOKING
10 min

SERVING
4

INGREDIENTS

- 1 lb. / 450g beef roast
- 4 cups beef broth
- 3 garlic cloves, chopped
- 1 carrot, chopped
- 2 celery stalks, chopped
- 2 tomatoes, chopped
- 1/2 white onion, chopped
- 1/4 teaspoon salt
- 1/8 teaspoon ground black pepper

DIRECTIONS

1. Add listed ingredients to your Ninja Foodi and lock lid, cook on "High" pressure for 10 minutes

2. Quick-release pressure. Open the lid and shred the bee using forks, serve, and enjoy!

Mediterranean Lamb Roast

PREPARATION
15 min

COOKING
50 min

SERVING
4

INGREDIENTS

- 2 tablespoons olive oil
- 5 lb. / 2.25 kg leg of lamb
- Salt and pepper to taste
- 1 teaspoon dried marjoram
- 3 cloves garlic, minced
- 1 teaspoon dried sage
- 1 teaspoon dried thyme
- 1 teaspoon ground ginger
- 1 bay leaf, crushed
- 2 cups broth
- 3 lb. / 1.35 kg potatoes, sliced into cubes
- 2 tablespoons arrowroot powder
- 1/3 cup water

DIRECTIONS

1. Set the Ninja Foodi to "Sauté". Pour in the olive oil. Add the lamb.
2. Coat with the oil. Season with the herbs and spices. Sear on both sides.
3. Pour in the broth. Add the potatoes. Close the pot. Set it to "Pressure".
4. Cook at "High" pressure for 50 minutes. Release the pressure naturally.
5. Dissolve the arrowroot powder in water.
6. Stir in the diluted arrowroot powder into the cooking liquid.
7. Let sit for a few minutes before serving.

Serving Suggestion:

Serve with cauliflowe rice.

Rosemary Lamb Chops

PREPARATION
10 min

COOKING
7 min

SERVING
4

INGREDIENTS

- 3 lb. / 1.35 kg lamb chops
- 4 rosemary sprigs
- Salt to taste
- 1 tablespoon olive oil
- 2 tablespoons butter
- 1 tablespoon tomato paste
- 1 cup beef stock
- 1 green onion, sliced

DIRECTIONS

1. Season the lamb chops with rosemary, salt, and pepper.
2. Pour in the olive oil and add the butter to the Ninja Foodi. Set it to "Sauté".
3. Add the lamb chops and cook for one minute per side. Add the rest of the ingredients.
4. Stir well. Cover the pot. Set it to "Pressure". Cook at "High" pressure for 5 minutes.
5. Release the pressure naturally.

Serving Suggestion:

Serve with pickled onions.

Braised Lamb Shanks

PREPARATION
20 min

COOKING
around **60** min

SERVING
4

INGREDIENTS

- 2 tablespoons olive oil
- 4 lamb shanks
- Salt and pepper to taste
- 4 cloves garlic, minced
- 3/4 cup dry red wine
- 1 teaspoon dried basil
- 3/4 teaspoons dried oregano
- 28 oz. / 800g crushed tomatoes

DIRECTIONS

1. Turn the Ninja Foodi to "Sauté". Add the oil. Season the lamb with salt and pepper.
2. Cook until brown. Remove and set aside. Add the garlic and cook for 15 seconds.
3. Pour in the wine. Simmer for 2 minutes. Stir in the basil, oregano, and tomatoes.
4. Put the lamb back in the pot. Seal the pot. Set it to "Pressure".
5. Cook at "High" pressure for 45 minutes. Release the pressure naturally.

Serving Suggestion:

Serve over polenta.

Simple/Aromatic Meatballs

PREPARATION
8 min

COOKING
11 min

SERVING
4

INGREDIENTS

- 2 cups ground beef
- 1 egg, beaten
- 1 teaspoon taco seasoning
- 1 tablespoon sugar-free marinara sauce
- 1 teaspoon garlic, minced
- 1/2 teaspoon salt

DIRECTIONS

1. Take a big mixing bowl and place all the ingredients into the bowl

2. Add all the ingredients into the bowl. Mix all the ingredients by using a spoon or fingertip Then make the small size meatballs and put them in a layer in the Cook & Crisp basket

3. Lower the Crisping lid. Cook the meatballs for 11 minutes at 350° F / 180° C. Serve immediately and enjoy it!

Generous Shepherd's Pie

PREPARATION
10 min

COOKING
15 min

SERVING
4

INGREDIENTS

- 2 cups of water
- 4 tablespoons butter
- 4 oz. / 115g cream cheese
- 1 cup mozzarella
- 1 whole egg
- Salt and pepper to taste
- 1 tablespoon garlic powder
- 3 lb. / 1.35 kg ground beef
- 1 cup frozen carrots
- 8 oz. / 225g mushrooms, sliced
- 1 cup beef broth

DIRECTIONS

1. Add water to Ninja Foodi, arrange cauliflowe on top, lock lid and cook for 5 minutes on "High" pressure. Quick-release and transfer to a blender, add cream cheese, butter, mozzarella cheese, egg, pepper, and salt. Blend well. Drain water from Ninja Foodi and add beef

2. Add carrots, garlic powder, broth and pepper, and salt

3. Add in cauliflowe mix and lock lid, cook for 10 minutes on "High" pressure

4. Release pressure naturally over 10 minutes. Serve and enjoy!

Lamb Curry

PREPARATION
5-10 min

COOKING
20 min

SERVING
4

INGREDIENTS

- 1 1/2 lb. / 700g lamb stew meat, cubed
- 1 tablespoon lime juice
- 4 cloves garlic, minced
- 1/2 cup coconut milk
- 1 inch / 2.5 cm piece fresh ginger, grated
- Salt and pepper to taste
- 1 tablespoon coconut oil
- 14 oz. / 400g diced tomatoes
- 3/4 teaspoon turmeric
- 1 tablespoon curry powder
- 1 onion, diced
- 3 carrots, sliced

DIRECTIONS

1. In a bowl, toss the lamb meat in lime juice, garlic, coconut milk, ginger, salt, and pepper. Marinate for 30 minutes.
2. Put the meat with its marinade and the rest of the ingredients in the Ninja Foodi.
3. Mix well. Seal the pot. Set it to "Pressure". Cook at "High" pressure for 20 minutes.
4. Release the pressure naturally.

Serving Suggestion:

Garnish with chopped cilantro.

Pear Fresh Pork

PREPARATION
15 min

COOKING
12 min

SERVING
6

INGREDIENTS

- 2 lb. / 900g pork tenderloin, ¾ inch / 2 cm slices
- 2 garlic cloves, minced
- 1 1/2 teaspoons ground cumin
- 1 1/2 teaspoons dried oregano
- 1/2 teaspoon black pepper
- 1/4 cup lime juice
- 2 tablespoons olive oil

Pear Mix:

- 1 jalapeno pepper, seeded and chopped
- 2 tablespoons lime juice
- 4 cups pears, chopped peeled
- 1 teaspoon sugar
- 1/3 cup chopped red onion
- 2 tablespoons chopped mint
- 1 tablespoon lime zest, grated
- 1/2 teaspoon black pepper

DIRECTIONS

1. Season the pork with lime juice, cumin, oregano, oil, garlic, and pepper in a bowl. Cover and refrigerate for 8 hours or overnight to marinate.

2. In a mixing bowl, add the pear mix ingredients. Combine the ingredients to mix well with each other.

3. Take Ninja Foodi, arrange it over your kitchen platform, and open the top lid. Arrange the Grill grate and close the top lid.

4. Press "Grill" and select the "High" grill function. Adjust the timer to 12 minutes and then press "Start/Stop." Ninja Foodi will start preheating.

5. Ninja Foodi is preheated and ready to cook when it starts to beep. After you hear a beep, open the top lid. Arrange the pork slices over the Grill grate.

6. Close the top lid and cook for 6 minutes. Now open the top lid, fli the pork slices.

7. Close the top lid and cook for 6 more minutes.

8. Serve the sliced pork warm with the pear mixture on top.

Tantalizing Beef Jerky

PREPARATION
10 min

COOKING
7 hour

SERVING
4

INGREDIENTS

- 1/2 lb. / 225g beef, sliced into 1/8 inch / 0.3 cm thick strips
- 1/2 cup of soy sauce
- 2 tablespoons Worcestershire sauce
- 2 teaspoons ground black pepper
- 1 teaspoon onion powder
- 1/2 teaspoon garlic powder
- 1 teaspoon salt

DIRECTIONS

1. Add listed ingredient to a large-sized Ziploc bag, seal it shut
2. Shake well, leave it in the fridge overnight
3. Lay strips on Dehydrating rack, making sure not to overlap them
4. Lock Crisping Lid and set the temperature to 135° F / 60° C, "Dehydrate" for 7 hours
5. Store in an airtight container, enjoy!

Cool Beef Bourguignon

PREPARATION
10 min

COOKING
30 min

SERVING
4

INGREDIENTS

- 1 lb. / 450g stewing steak
- 1/2 lb. / 225g bacon
- 5 medium carrots, diced
- 1 large red onion, peeled and sliced
- 2 garlic cloves, minced
- 2 teaspoons salt
- 2 tablespoons fresh thyme
- 2 tablespoons fresh parsley
- 2 teaspoons ground pepper
- 1/2 cup beef broth
- 1 tablespoon olive oil
- 1 tablespoon sugar-free maple syrup (Keto friendly)

DIRECTIONS

1. Set your Ninja Foodi to "Sauté" mode and add 1 tablespoon of oil, allow the oil to heat up
2. Pat your beef dry and season it well
3. Add beef into the Ninja Foodi (in batches) and Sauté them until nicely browned up
4. Slice up the cooked bacon into strips and add the strips to the pot
5. Add onions as well and brown them
6. Add the rest of the listed ingredients and lock up the lid
7. Cook for 30 minutes on "High" pressure
8. Allow the pressure to release naturally over 10 minutes. Enjoy!

A Keto-Friendly Philly Willy Steak and Cheese

PREPARATION
10 min

COOKING
40 min

SERVING
4

INGREDIENTS

- 2 tablespoons olive oil
- 2 large onion, sliced
- 8 oz. / 225g mushrooms, sliced
- 1-2 teaspoons Keto-friendly steak seasoning
- 1 tablespoon butter
- 2 lb. / 900g beef chuck roast
- 12 cup beef stock

DIRECTIONS

1. Set your Ninja Foodi to "Sauté" mode and add oil, let it heat up
2. Rub seasoning over roast and Sauté for 1-2 minutes per side
3. Remove and add butter, onion
4. Add mushrooms, pepper, stock, and roast
5. Lock lid and cook on "High" pressure for 35 minutes
6. Naturally, release the pressure over 10 minutes
7. Shred meat and sprinkle cheese if using, enjoy!

Onion Beef Roast

PREPARATION
5-10 min

COOKING
30 min

SERVING
6

INGREDIENTS

- 2 sticks of celery, sliced
- 1 bulb of garlic, peeled and crushed
- A bunch of herbs of your choice
- 2 lb. / 900g topside of beef
- 2 medium onions, chopped
- Salt and ground black pepper to taste
- 1 tablespoon butter
- 3 tablespoons olive oil

DIRECTIONS

1. In a mixing bowl, add the ingredients. Combine the ingredients to mix well with each other.

2. Take Ninja Foodi, arrange it over your kitchen platform, and open the top lid. Lightly grease the cooking pot with some oil or cooking spray.

3. Press "Roast" and adjust the temperature to 380° F / 195° C. Adjust the timer to 30 minutes and then press "Start/Stop." Ninja Foodi will start preheating.

4. Ninja Foodi is preheated and ready to cook when it starts to beep. After you hear a beep, open the top lid.

5. Arrange the bowl mixture directly inside the pot.

6. Close the top lid and allow it to cook until the timer reads zero.

7. Serve warm.

Kale Sausage Soup

PREPARATION
5-10 min

COOKING
10 min

SERVING
4

INGREDIENTS

- ½ diced onion
- 2 cup chicken broth
- 1 lb. / 450g chopped sausage roll
- 1 tablespoon olive oil
- 2 cup almond milk
- ½ cup parmesan cheese
- 3 cup chopped kale fresh
- 28 oz. / 800g tomatoes, crushed
- 1 tablespoon minced garlic
- 1 teaspoon oregano, dried
- ¼ teaspoon salt

DIRECTIONS

1. Select "Sauté" mode and select "MD: HI" pressure level. Press "Start/ Stop" After about 4-5 minutes, the unit is ready to cook.

2. Add the sausage and stir-cook to brown evenly. Add the spices, onions, kale, tomatoes, milk, and chicken broth. Stir the mixture.

3. Seal the multi-cooker by locking it with the pressure lid; ensure to keep the pressure release valve locked/ sealed.

4. Select "Pressure" mode and select the "Hi" pressure level. Then, set the timer to 10 minutes and press "Start/Stop"; it will start the cooking process by building up inside pressure.

5. When the timer goes off naturally release inside pressure for about 8-10 minutes. Then, quick-release pressure by adjusting the pressure valve to the "Vent". Serve warm with the cheese on top and enjoy!

Juiciest Keto Bacon Strips

PREPARATION
5 min

COOKING
8 min

SERVING
2

INGREDIENTS

- 10 bacon strips
- 1/4 teaspoon chili flake
- 1/3 teaspoon salt
- 1/4 teaspoon basil, dried

DIRECTIONS

1. Rub the bacon strips with chili flakes dried basil, and salt

2. Turn on your Ninja Foodi and place the bacon on the Reversible rack

3. Close the Crisping lid. Cook the bacon at 400° F / 205° C for 5 minutes

4. Cook for 3 minutes more if the bacon is not fully cooked. Serve and enjoy!

Hybrid Beef Prime Roast

PREPARATION
10 min

COOKING
45 min

SERVING
4

INGREDIENTS

- 2 lb. / 900g chuck roast
- 1 tablespoon olive oil
- 1 teaspoon salt
- 1 teaspoon ground black pepper
- 1 teaspoon onion powder
- 1 teaspoon garlic powder
- 4 cups beef stock

DIRECTIONS

1. Place roast in Ninja Food Removable Cooking pot and season it well with salt and pepper

2. Add oil and set the pot to "Sauté" mode, sear each side of the roast for 3 minutes until lightly browned

3. Add beef broth, onion powder, garlic powder, and stir

4. Lock lid and cook on "High" pressure for 40 minutes

5. Once the timer goes off naturally release the pressure over 10 minutes

6. Open the lid and serve hot. Enjoy!

The Epic Carne Guisada

PREPARATION
10 min

COOKING
30 min

SERVING
4

INGREDIENTS

- 3 lb. / 1.35 kg beef stew
- 3 tablespoon seasoned salt
- 1 tablespoon oregano chili powder
- 1 tablespoon organic cumin
- 1 pinch crushed red pepper
- 2 tablespoons olive oil
- 1/2 medium lime, juiced
- 1 cup beef bone broth
- 3 oz. / 85g tomato paste
- 1 large onion, sliced

DIRECTIONS

1. Trim the beef stew as needed into small bite-sized portions
2. Toss the beef stew pieces with dry seasoning
3. Set your Ninja Foodi to "Sauté" mode and add oil, allow the oil to heat up
4. Add seasoned beef pieces and brown them
5. Combine the browned beef pieces with the rest of the ingredients
6. Lock up the lid and cook on "High" pressure for 30 minutes
7. Release the pressure naturally
8. Enjoy!

No-Noodle Pure Lasagna

PREPARATION
10 min

COOKING
10 min

SERVING
4

INGREDIENTS

- 2 small onions
- 2 garlic cloves, minced
- 1 lb. / 450g ground beef
- 1 large egg
- 1 and 1/2 cups ricotta cheese
- 1/2 cup parmesan cheese
- 1 jar 25 oz. / 700g (marinara sauce)
- 8 oz. / 225g mozzarella cheese, sliced

DIRECTIONS

1. Set your Ninja Foodi to "Sauté" mode add beef, brown the beef
2. Add onion and garlic
3. Add parmesan, ricotta, egg in a small dish and keep it on the side
4. Add sauce to browned meat, reserve half for later
5. Sprinkle mozzarella and half of ricotta cheese to the browned meat
6. Top with remaining meat sauce
7. For the final layer, add more mozzarella cheese and remaining ricotta
8. Stir well
9. Cover with a foil transfer to Ninja Foodi
10. Lock lid and cook on "High" pressure for 10 minutes
11. Quick-release pressure
12. Drizzle parmesan cheese on top
13. Enjoy!

Spinach Beef Meatloaf

PREPARATION
5-10 min

COOKING
70 min

SERVING
6

INGREDIENTS

- ¼ cup tomato puree or crushed tomatoes
- 1 oz. / 450g lean ground beef
- ½ cup onion, chopped
- 2 garlic cloves, minced
- ½ cup green bell pepper, seeded and chopped
- 2 eggs, beaten
- 1 cup cheddar cheese, grated
- 3 cups spinach, chopped
- 1 teaspoon dried thyme, crushed
- 6 cups mozzarella cheese, grated
- Black pepper to taste

DIRECTIONS

1. In a blending bowl, include the entirety of the listed ingredients except for cheese and spinach.

2. Place the mixture over a wax paper; top with spinach, cheese, and roll it to form a nice meatloaf. Remove wax paper and add the mixture in the baking pan.

3. In the pot, add water and place a reversible rack inside the pot. Place the pan over the rack.

4. Seal the multi-cooker by locking it with the crisping lid; ensure to keep the pressure release valve locked/sealed.

5. Select "Bake/Roast" mode and adjust the 380° F / 195° C temperature level. Then, set the timer to 70 minutes and press "Start/Stop"; it will start the cooking process by building up inside pressure.

6. At the point when the clock goes off fast discharge pressure by adjusting the pressure valve to the "Vent". After pressure gets released, open the pressure lid.

7. Serve warm.

CHAPTER 12

Beef and Lamb Recipes

Steak with Asparagus

PREPARATION
20 min

COOKING
20 min

SERVING
4

INGREDIENTS

- 2 strip steaks
- 2 tablespoons vegetable oil, divided
- Pinch steak seasoning
- Salt and pepper to taste
- 2 cups asparagus, trimmed and sliced

DIRECTIONS

1. Coat strip steaks with half of the oil.
2. Season with steak seasoning, salt, and pepper.
3. Toss asparagus with oil, salt, and pepper.
4. Add Grill grate to the Ninja Foodi. Seal the hood.
5. Select the "Grill" function and preheat it on "High" for 10 minutes.
6. Add steaks to the grill.
7. Cook for 5 minutes.
8. Flip and cook for 5 more minutes.
9. Add asparagus to the veggie tray.
10. Place the veggie tray on top of the grill grate.
11. Cook for 10 minutes.
12. Serve steak with asparagus.

Serving Suggestions:

Serve with salad or brown rice.

Tips:

Press steaks onto the grill to give it grill marks.

Grilled Pork Chops

PREPARATION
10 min

COOKING
15 min

SERVING
4

INGREDIENTS

- 4 pork chops
- Salt and pepper to taste
- Barbecue sauce

DIRECTIONS

1. Add a Grill grate to your Ninja Foodi.
2. Set it to "Grill". Close the hood.
3. Preheat it on "High" for 15 minutes.
4. Season pork chops with salt and pepper.
5. Add to the Grill grates.
6. Grill for 8 minutes.
7. Flip and cook for another 7 minutes, brushing both sides with barbecue sauce.

Serving Suggestions:

Let rest for 5 minutes before slicing and serving.

Tips:

You can also make your barbecue sauce by mixing soy sauce, sugar or honey, lemon juice, and ketchup.

Roast Beef with Garlic

PREPARATION
10 min

COOKING
70 min

SERVING
4

INGREDIENTS

- 2 lb. / 900g beef roast, sliced
- 2 tablespoons vegetable oil
- Salt and pepper to taste
- 6 cloves garlic

DIRECTIONS

1. Coat beef roast with oil.
2. Season with salt and pepper.
3. Place inside the Ninja Foodi Removable Cooking pot.
4. Sprinkle garlic on top.
5. Choose a "Bake" setting.
6. Set it to 400° F / 205° C and cook for 30 minutes.
7. Reduce temperature to 375° F / 190° C and cook for another 40 minutes.

Serving Suggestions:

Serve with mashed potato and gravy.

Tips:

If refrigerated, let beef come to room temperature 2 hours before cooking.

Grilled Steak & Potatoes

PREPARATION
10 min

COOKING
50 min

SERVING
4

INGREDIENTS

- 4 potatoes
- 3 sirloin steaks
- 1/4 cup avocado oil
- 2 tablespoons steak seasoning
- Salt to taste

DIRECTIONS

1. Poke potatoes with a fork.
2. Coat potatoes with half of the avocado oil.
3. Season with salt.
4. Add to the Cook & Crisp basket.
5. Choose the "Air Fry" function in your Ninja Foodi.
6. Seal the hood and cook at 400° F / 205° C for 35 minutes.
7. Flip and cook for another 10 minutes.
8. Transfer to a plate.
9. Add Grill grate to the Ninja Foodi.
10. Add steaks to the Grill grate.
11. Set it to "Grill" at "High".
12. Cook for 7 minutes per side.
13. Serve steaks with potatoes.

Serving Suggestions:

Serve with steak sauce and hot sauce.

Tips:

Press steaks onto the grill to give it grill marks.

Cuban Pork Chops

PREPARATION
20 min

COOKING
15 min

SERVING
4

INGREDIENTS

- 4 pork chops
- 1/2 cup olive oil
- 8 cloves garlic, minced
- 1 cup orange juice
- 1/2 cup lime juice
- 1 teaspoon orange zest
- 1 teaspoon lime zest
- 1/4 cup mint leaves, chopped
- 2 teaspoons dried oregano
- 2 teaspoons ground cumin
- 1 cup cilantro, chopped

DIRECTIONS

1. Place pork chops in a shallow plate.
2. In another bowl, mix the remaining ingredients.
3. Take ¼ cup of the mixture and set aside.
4. Add the remaining mixture to the pork chops.
5. Cover and marinate in the refrigerator for 8 hours.
6. Add Grill grate to the Ninja Foodi. Seal the hood.
7. Choose a "Grill" setting.
8. Set it to "High".
9. Set the time to 15 minutes.
10. Close the hood and cook for 15 minutes, flippin once.

Serving Suggestions:

Let rest for 5 minutes before slicing and serving.

Tips:

You can also marinate only for 1 hour if you want a shorter preparation time.

Beef Stew

PREPARATION
10 min

COOKING
10 min

SERVING
4

INGREDIENTS

- 1 lb. / 450g beef roast
- 1 carrot, chopped
- 2 celery stalks, chopped
- 4 cups beef broth
- 3 garlic cloves, chopped
- ½ white onion, chopped
- 2 tomatoes, chopped
- ¼ teaspoon salt
- 1/8 teaspoon ground black pepper

DIRECTIONS

1. Add all the listed ingredients to your Ninja Foodi
2. Close the lid
3. Cook on "High" pressure for 10 minutes
4. Quick-release the pressure
5. Open the lid and shred the beef using forks
6. Serve and enjoy!

Romantic Mustard Pork

PREPARATION
10 min

COOKING
30 min

SERVING
4

INGREDIENTS

- 2 tablespoons butter
- 2 tablespoons Dijon mustard (Keto-Friendly)
- 4 pork chops
- Salt and pepper to taste
- 1 tablespoon fresh rosemary, coarsely chopped

DIRECTIONS

1. Take a bowl and add pork chops, cover with Dijon mustard and carefully sprinkle rosemary, salt, and pepper. Let it marinate for 2 hours

2. Add butter and marinated pork chops to your Ninja Foodi Removable Cooking pot

3. Lock lid and cook on "Low-Md" Pressure for 30 minutes

4. Release pressure naturally over 10 minutes. Take the dish out, serve, and enjoy!

Roast Beef & Grilled Potatoes

PREPARATION
15 min

COOKING
45 min

SERVING
6

INGREDIENTS

- 2 1/2 teaspoons onion powder
- 2 1/2 teaspoons garlic powder
- Salt and pepper to taste
- 3 lb. / 1.35 kg top round roast
- 4 cups potatoes, grilled

DIRECTIONS

1. Combine onion powder, garlic powder, salt, and pepper in a bowl.
2. Rub top round roast with dry rub.
3. Set the Ninja Foodi to "Broil".
4. Preheat it on "High" for 10 minutes.
5. Add the roast beef and cook for 25 minutes.
6. Turn and cook for another 20 minutes.
7. Serve with grilled potatoes.

Serving Suggestions:
Slice against the grain and serve.

Tips:
Let the roast come to room temperature for 1 hour before seasoning.

Grilled Herbed Steak

PREPARATION
5 min

COOKING
10 min

SERVING
4

INGREDIENTS

- 4 steaks
- Garlic salt to taste
- 4 sprigs rosemary, chopped
- 1 teaspoon dried tarragon
- 1 teaspoon dried basil

DIRECTIONS

1. Add grill grate to the Ninja Foodi.
2. Close the hood and choose a "Grill" setting.
3. Set it to 10 minutes.
4. Set it to "High".
5. Press "Start/Stop" to preheat.
6. Rub both sides of steak with garlic salt.
7. Sprinkle with herbs.
8. Add steaks to the grill grate.
9. Cook for 5 minutes per side.

Serving Suggestions:

Garnish with fresh rosemary sprig.

Tips:

Marinate steak in herbs for 15 minutes before cooking.

Creative and Easy Lamb Roast

PREPARATION
10 min

COOKING
55 min

SERVING
6

INGREDIENTS

- 2 lb. / 900g lamb roast
- 1 cup onion soup
- 1 cup beef broth
- Salt and pepper to taste

DIRECTIONS

1. Transfer lamb roast to your Ninja Foodi Removable Cooking pot. Add onion soup, beef broth, salt, and pepper

2. Lock lid and cook on "MD:HI" pressure for 55 minutes

3. Release pressure naturally over 10 minutes. Transfer to a serving bowl, serve and enjoy!

CHAPTER 13

Appetizers, Sides, and Snacks

Bacon Brussels Delight

PREPARATION
7 min

COOKING
12 min

SERVING
4

INGREDIENTS

- 6 slices bacon, chopped
- 1 lb. / 450g Brussels sprouts halved
- 1/2 teaspoon black pepper
- 1 tablespoon of sea salt
- 2 tablespoons olive oil, extra-virgin

DIRECTIONS

1. Take a mixing bowl and toss the Brussels sprouts, olive oil, bacon, salt, and black pepper
2. Arrange the Cook & Crip basket inside the pot
3. Preheat Ninja Foodi by selecting "Air Fry" at 390° F / 200° C and timer to 12 minutes
4. Let it preheat until you hear a beep
5. Arrange the Brussels sprout mixture directly inside the basket
6. Close the top lid and cook for 6 minutes, then shake the basket
7. Close the top lid and cook for 6 minutes more
8. Serve warm and enjoy!

Crispy Potato Cubes

PREPARATION
10 min

COOKING
15 min

SERVING
4

INGREDIENTS

- 1 lb. / 450g potato, peeled
- 1 tablespoon olive oil
- 1 teaspoon dried dill
- 1 teaspoon dried oregano
- 1/4 teaspoon chili flake

DIRECTIONS

1. Preheat Ninja Foodi by selecting the "Air Fry", set it to 400° F / 205° C and timer to 15 minutes
2. Let it preheat until you hear a beep
3. Cut potatoes into cubes
4. Sprinkle potato cubes with dill, oregano, and chili flakes
5. Transfer into Ninja Foodi Cook & Crisp basket and cook for 15 minutes
6. Stir while cooking, once they are crunchy
7. Serve and enjoy!

Crazy Fresh Onion Soup

PREPARATION
5 min

COOKING
25 min

SERVING
4

INGREDIENTS

- 2 tablespoons avocado oil
- 8 cups yellow onion
- 1 tablespoon balsamic vinegar
- 6 cups of pork stock
- 1 teaspoon salt
- 2 bay leaves
- 2 large sprigs, fresh thyme

DIRECTIONS

1. Cut up the onion in half through the root
2. Peel them and slice into thin half-moons
3. Set the pot to "Sauté" mode and add oil, once the oil is hot and add onions
4. Cook for about 15 minutes
5. Add balsamic vinegar and scrape any from the bottom
6. Add stock, bay leaves, salt, and thyme
7. Lock up the lid and cook on "High" pressure for 10 minutes
8. Release the pressure naturally
9. Discard the bay leaf and thyme stems
10. Blend the soup using an immersion blender and serve!

Healthy Onion Rings

PREPARATION
10 min

COOKING
10 min

SERVING
4

INGREDIENTS

- 1/4 teaspoon salt
- 1 egg
- 3/4 cup milk
- 1 tablespoon baking powder
- 3/4 cup breadcrumbs
- 1 large onion
- 1 cup flou
- 1 teaspoon paprika

DIRECTIONS

1. Preheat Ninja Foodi by selecting "Air Fry", set it to 340° F / 170° C and timer to 10 minutes
2. Let it preheat until you hear a beep
3. Take a bowl and whisk the egg, milk, salt, flour paprika together
4. Slice the onion and separate into rings
5. Grease your Ninja Foodi with cooking spray
6. Then dip the onion rings into batter and coat with breadcrumbs
7. Arrange them in Ninja Foodi Cook & Crisp basket
8. Cook for 10 minutes
9. Serve and enjoy!

Hearty Ninja Food Bean

PREPARATION
5 min

COOKING
10 min

SERVING
4

INGREDIENTS

- Fresh ground black pepper
- Flaky sea salt
- Pinch of pepper
- 1 lemon, juiced
- 2 tablespoon oil
- 1 lb. / 450g green bean, trimmed

DIRECTIONS

1. Take a medium bowl and add the green bean
2. Mix and stir well
3. Select "Grill"at "Max", set the timer to 10 minutes and preheat
4. Wait until you hear a beep
5. Transfer beans to the Grill grate, cook for 10 minutes
6. Toss well to ensure that all sides cooked evenly
7. Squeeze a bit of lemon juice on top
8. Season with salt, pepper, and pepper flakes according to your taste
9. Enjoy!

Seared Tuna Salad

PREPARATION
10 min

COOKING
6 min

SERVING
4

INGREDIENTS

- 1/2 lb. / 225g ahi tuna, cut into four strips
- 2 tablespoons sesame oil
- 1(10 oz. / 280g) bag baby greens
- 2 tablespoons of rice wine vinegar
- 6 tablespoons extra-virgin olive oil
- 1/2 English cucumber, sliced
- 1/4 teaspoon of sea salt
- 1/2 teaspoon ground black pepper

DIRECTIONS

1. Supplement the flam broil mesh and close the hood
2. Preheat Ninja Foodi by pressing the "Grill" option at and setting it to "Max" and timer to 6 minutes
3. Take a small bowl, whisk together the rice vinegar, salt, and pepper
4. Slowly pour in the oil while whisking until vinaigrette is fully combined
5. Season the fis with salt and pepper, sprinkle with the sesame oil
6. Once it preheats until you hear a beep
7. Arrange the shrimp over the Grill grate lock lid and cook for 6 minutes
8. Do not fli during cooking
9. Once cooked completely, top salad with tuna strip
10. Drizzle the vinaigrette over the top
11. Serve immediately and enjoy!

Great Mac and Cheese Bowl

PREPARATION
10 min

COOKING
25 min

SERVING
4

INGREDIENTS

- 1 tablespoon parmesan cheese, grated
- Salt and pepper to taste
- 1 ½ cup cheddar cheese, grated
- ½ cup warm milk
- ½ cup broccoli
- 1 cup elbow macaroni

DIRECTIONS

1. Preheat your Ninja Foodi to 400° F / 205° C in "Air Fry" mode, set timer to 10 minutes
2. Once you hear the beep, it is preheated
3. Take a pot and add water, bring the water to a boil
4. Add macaroni and veggies, boil for 10 minutes until cooked
5. Drain pasta and veggies, toss pasta and veggies with cheese and sauce
6. Season well with salt and pepper and transfer to Ninja Foodi
7. Sprinkle more cheese on top and cook for 15 minutes
8. Take it out and let it cool for 10 minutes
9. Serve and enjoy!

Lemon-Garlic Shrimp Caesar Salad

PREPARATION
10 min

COOKING
5 min

SERVING
4

INGREDIENTS

- 1 lb. / 450g fresh jumbo shrimp
- 2 heads romaine lettuce, chopped
- 3/4 cup Caesar dressing
- 1/2 cup parmesan cheese, grated
- 1/2 lemon juice
- 3 garlic cloves, minced
- Sea salt
- Black pepper, grounded

DIRECTIONS

1. Preheat Ninja Foodi by pressing "Grill" option, set it to "Max" and timer to 5 minutes
2. Take a large bowl; toss the shrimp with the lemon juice, garlic, salt, and pepper
3. Let it marinate while the grill is preheating
4. Once it preheats until you hear a beep
5. Arrange the shrimp over the grill grate lock lid and cook for 5 minutes
6. Toss the romaine lettuce with the Caesar dressing
7. Once cooked completely, remove the shrimp from the grill
8. Sprinkle with parmesan cheese
9. Serve and enjoy!

Healthy Granola Bites

PREPARATION
10 min

COOKING
20 min

SERVING
4

INGREDIENTS

- Salt and pepper to taste
- 1 tablespoon coriander
- A handful of thyme, diced
- ¼ cup of coconut milk
- 3 handful of cooked vegetables, your choice
- 3 oz. /85g plain granola

DIRECTIONS

1. Preheat your Ninja Foodi to 355° F / 180° C in "Air Fry" mode, set timer to 20 minutes
2. Take a bowl and add your cooked vegetables, granola
3. Use an immersion blender to blitz your granola until you have a nice breadcrumb-like consistency
4. Add coconut milk to the mix and mix until you have a nice fir texture
5. Use the mixture to make granola balls and transfer them into Ninja Foodi
6. Cook for 20 minutes
7. Serve and enjoy!

Cheese Dredged Cauliflower Snack

PREPARATION
10 min

COOKING
33 min

SERVING
4

INGREDIENTS

- 1 head cauliflowe
- ¼ cup butter, cut into small pieces
- ½ cup parmesan cheese, grated
- 1 teaspoon avocado mayonnaise
- 1 tablespoon mustard

DIRECTIONS

1. Set your Ninja Foodi to "Sauté" mode and add butter and cauliflowe
2. Sauté for 3 minutes
3. Add rest of the ingredients
4. Give it a nice stir
5. Close the lid
6. Cook on "High" pressure for 30 minutes
7. Release pressure naturally over 10 minutes
8. Serve and enjoy!

Honey Roasted Carrots

PREPARATION
5 min

COOKING
12 min

SERVING
4

INGREDIENTS

- 3 cups carrots, sliced into chunks
- 1 tablespoon olive oil
- 1 tablespoon honey
- Salt and pepper to taste

DIRECTIONS

1. Coat the carrots with the olive oil and honey.
2. Season with the salt and pepper.
3. Put in the Ninja Foodi Cook & Crisp basket.
4. Cover with the crisping lid.
5. Set it to "Air Fry".
6. Cook at 350° F / 180° C for 12 minutes.

Serving Suggestion:

Sprinkle herbs on top.

Roasted Corn

PREPARATION
6 min

COOKING
10 min

SERVING
4

INGREDIENTS

- 4 ears of corn, husks removed and sliced into 2
- 2 teaspoons olive oil
- Salt and pepper to taste

DIRECTIONS

1. Coat the corn with oil and season with salt and pepper.
2. Put in the Ninja Foodi Cook & Crisp basket.
3. Seal with the crisping lid.
4. Set it to "Air Fry".
5. Cook at 400° F / 205°C for 10 minutes.

Serving Suggestion:

Sprinkle Parmesan cheese or brush with butter.

Sweet Potato

PREPARATION
10 min

COOKING
40 min

SERVING
4

INGREDIENTS

- 3 sweet potatoes, washed and poked with fork 1 tablespoon olive oil
- Salt and pepper to taste

DIRECTIONS

1. Coat the sweet potato with olive oil.
2. Season with the salt and pepper.
3. Place in the Ninja Foodi Cook & Crisp basket.
4. Seal with the crisping lid.
5. Choose the "Air Fry" function.
6. Cook at 390° F / 200° C for 40 minutes.

Lemon Parmesan Broccoli

PREPARATION
10 min

COOKING
19 min

SERVING
4

INGREDIENTS

- 6 cups water
- 2 lb. / 900g broccoli floret
- 2 tablespoons olive oil
- Salt and pepper to taste
- 1/4 cup Kalamata olives, pitted and sliced in half
- 2 teaspoons lemon zest, grated
- 1/4 cup Parmesan cheese, grated

DIRECTIONS

1. Fill the Ninja Foodi with water.
2. Set it to "Sauté".
3. Let the water boil.
4. Add the broccoli and cook for 4 minutes.
5. Drain the water.
6. Toss the broccoli in olive oil and season with the salt and pepper.
7. Place in the basket and seal with the crisping lid.
8. Choose the "Air Fry" function.
9. Cook at 400° F / 2005° C for 15 minutes.
10. Flip halfway through.
11. Toss the broccoli in the lemon zest and Parmesan cheese and mix with the olives.

Serving Suggestion:

Serve with pasta or soup.

Mozzarella Sticks and Grilled Eggplant

PREPARATION
10 min

COOKING
14 min

SERVING
4

INGREDIENTS

- Salt as needed
- ½ lb. / 225g buffal mozzarella, sliced into ¼ inch / 0.7 cm thick
- 12 large basil leaves
- 2 heirloom tomatoes, sliced into ¼ inch / 0.7 cm thickness
- 2 tablespoon canola oil
- 1 eggplant, ¼ inch / 0.7 cm thick

DIRECTIONS

1. Take a large bowl and add the eggplant, add oil and toss well until coated well
2. Preheat your Ninja Foodi to "Grill" at "Max" and set the timer to 14 minutes
3. Once you hear the beeping sound, transfer the prepared eggplants to your Grill grate and cook for 12 minutes until the surface is charred
4. Top with cheese slice, tomato, and mozzarella
5. Cook for 2 minutes, letting the cheese melt
6. Remove from grill and place 2-3 basil leaves on top of half stack
7. Place remaining eggplant stack on top alongside basil
8. Season well with salt and rest of the basil

Mediterranean Spinach

PREPARATION
10 min

COOKING
15 min

SERVING
4

INGREDIENTS

- 2 lb. / 900g spinach, chopped and boiled
- 4 tablespoons butter
- 2/3 cup Kalamata olives, halved and pitted
- 4 teaspoons fresh lemon zest, grated
- 1 ½ cups feta cheese, grated
- Salt and pepper to taste

DIRECTIONS

1. Add spinach, butter, salt, pepper into a bowl
2. Mix them well
3. Transfer to Ninja Foodi the seasoned spinach
4. Seal your Crisping Lid
5. "Air Fry" for 15 minutes at 350° F / 180° C
6. Serve and enjoy!

Garlic Mashed Potatoes

PREPARATION
8 min

COOKING
8 min

SERVING
4

INGREDIENTS

- 2 lb. / 900g potatoes, sliced into cubes
- 6 cloves garlic, crushed
- 2/3 cup chicken stock
- Salt and pepper to taste
- 3 tablespoons butter, divided
- 1/4 cup sour cream
- 1/4 cup cream cheese

DIRECTIONS

1. Place the potatoes inside the Ninja Foodi.
2. Add the chicken stock, garlic, salt, pepper, and 1/2 tablespoon butter.
3. Seal the pot.
4. Set it to "Pressure".
5. Cook at "High" pressure for 8 minutes.
6. Release the pressure naturally.
7. Mash the potatoes and stir in the rest of the ingredients and the remaining butter.

Serving Suggestion:

Garnish with chopped chives.

Fried Carrots, Zucchini and Squash

PREPARATION
10 min

COOKING
35 min

SERVING
4

INGREDIENTS

- 1/2 lb. / 225g carrots, cubed
- 6 teaspoons olive oil, divided
- 1 lb. / 450g zucchini, sliced into rounds
- 1 lb. /450g squash, sliced into half-moons
- Salt and pepper to taste
- 1 teaspoon dried tarragon

DIRECTIONS

1. Toss the carrots in 2 teaspoons of olive oil.
2. Place these in the Ninja Foodi Cook & Crisp basket.
3. Seal the crisping lid.
4. Choose the "Air Fry" function.
5. Cook at 400° F / 205° C for 5 minutes.
6. While waiting, drizzle the zucchini and squash in the remaining olive oil.
7. Season with the salt and pepper.
8. Add the zucchini and squash in the basket.
9. Cook at 400° F / 205° C for 30 minutes.
10. Season with the tarragon.

Serving Suggestion:

Garnish with chopped parsley.

Garlic Mushrooms

PREPARATION
5 min

COOKING
20 min

SERVING
4

INGREDIENTS

- 1 lb. / 450g mushrooms, rinsed and drained
- 1 teaspoon onion powder
- Black pepper to taste
- 1 tablespoon minced garlic
- 2 teaspoons soy sauce

DIRECTIONS

1. Mix all the ingredients in a bowl.
2. Put in the Ninja Foodi Cook & Crisp basket.
3. Seal the Crisping lid.
4. Set it to "Air Fry".
5. Cook at 360° F / 180° C for 20 minutes.
6. Coat the beef cubes with the salt and pickling spice.
7. In a skillet over medium heat, pour in the olive oil.

Serving Suggestion:

Sprinkle with chopped parsley.

Tips:

Use low sodium soy sauce.

Mediterranean Vegetables

PREPARATION
8 min

COOKING
15 min

SERVING
4

INGREDIENTS

- 1 cup cherry tomatoes
- 1 eggplant, sliced into rounds
- 1 green bell pepper, sliced into strips
- 1 carrot, sliced into rounds
- 1 teaspoon mixed herbs
- 6 tablespoons olive oil
- 2 tablespoons honey
- 1 teaspoon mustard
- 2 teaspoons garlic puree
- Salt and pepper to taste

DIRECTIONS

1. Drizzle the vegetables with the olive oil.
2. Add to the Ninja Foodi Cook & Crisp basket.
3. Seal the Crisping lid.
4. Set it to "Air Fry".
5. Cook at 360° F / 180° C for 15 minutes.
6. Mix the rest of the ingredients.
7. Pour the sauce over the vegetables before serving.

Serving Suggestion:

Garnish with lemon wedges.

Portobello and Pesto Sliders

PREPARATION
10 min

COOKING
8 min

SERVING
4

INGREDIENTS

- 8 small Portobello mushrooms, trimmed with gills removed
- 1 tomato, sliced
- 2 tablespoons canola oil
- 1/2 cup pesto
- 1/2 cup microgreens
- 2 tablespoons balsamic vinegar
- 8 slider buns

DIRECTIONS

1. Preheat Ninja Foodi by pressing the "Grill" option, set it to "High" and timer to 8 minutes
2. Brush the mushrooms with oil and balsamic vinegar
3. Once it preheats until you hear a beep
4. Arrange the mushrooms over the Grill grate lock lid and cook for 8 minutes
5. Once cooked, removed the mushrooms from the grill and layer on the buns with tomato, pesto, and microgreens
6. Serve immediately and enjoy!

Peanut Butter & Banana Snacks

PREPARATION
15 min

COOKING
9 min

SERVING
4

INGREDIENTS

- 1 cup peanut butter
- 8 slices whole-wheat bread
- 1 cup jam
- 2 bananas, sliced
- 2 teaspoons ground cinnamon
- 1/4 cup white sugar
- Cooking spray

DIRECTIONS

1. Spread peanut butter on 4 bread slices.
2. Spread jam on the remaining bread slices.
3. Add bananas and make 4 sandwiches.
4. In a bowl, mix cinnamon and sugar.
5. Select "Air Fry" function in your Ninja Foodi.
6. Set it to 390° F / 200° C for 6 minutes and preheat.
7. Add a crisper pan into the Ninja Foodi.
8. Spray sandwiches with oil and sprinkle with cinnamon mixture.
9. Air fry sandwiches for 6 minutes.
10. Flip and cook for 3 more minutes.

Serving Suggestions:

Serve with chocolate hazelnut spread.

Tips:

Use creamy peanut butter for this recipe.

Crispy Rosemary Potatoes

PREPARATION
10 min

COOKING
20-25 min

SERVING
4

INGREDIENTS

- 2 lb. / 900g baby red potatoes, quartered
- 2 tablespoons extra virgin olive oil
- 1/4 cup dried onion flake
- 1/2 teaspoon onion powder
- 1/2 teaspoon garlic powder
- 1/4 teaspoon celery powder
- 1/4 teaspoon freshly ground black pepper
- 1/2 teaspoon dried parsley
- 1/2 teaspoon salt

DIRECTIONS

1. Take a large bowl and add all listed ingredients, toss well and coat them well
2. Preheat Ninja Foodi by selecting "Air Fry", set to 390° F / 200° C and timer to 20 minutes
3. Let it preheat until you hear a beep
4. Once preheated, add potatoes to Cook & Crisp basket
5. Lock and cook for 10 minutes, making sure to shake the basket and cook for 10 minutes more
6. Once done, check the crispiness, if it's alright, serve away.
7. If not, cook for 5 minutes more
8. Enjoy!

Ranch Chicken Fingers

PREPARATION
15 min

COOKING
20 min

SERVING
4

INGREDIENTS

- 2 lb. / 900g chicken breast fillet sliced into strips
- 1 tablespoon olive oil
- 1 oz. / 28g ranch dressing seasoning mix
- 4 cups breadcrumbs
- Salt to taste

DIRECTIONS

1. Coat chicken strips with olive oil.
2. Sprinkle all sides with ranch seasoning.
3. Cover with foil and refrigerate for 1 to 2 hours.
4. In a bowl, mix breadcrumbs and salt.
5. Dredge the chicken strips with seasoned breadcrumbs.
6. Add Crisper pan to the Ninja Foodi.
7. Choose an "Air Fry" setting.
8. Set it to 390° F / 200° C.
9. Preheat for 3 minutes.
10. Add chicken strips to the crisper plate.
11. Cook for 20 minutes, flipping halfway through.

Serving Suggestions:

Serve with ketchup and mayo.

Tips:

Arrange chicken strips on the Crisper pan on a single layer.

Homemade Fries

PREPARATION
15 min

COOKING
45 min

SERVING
6

INGREDIENTS

- 1 lb. / 450g large potatoes, sliced into strips
- 2 tablespoons vegetable oil
- Salt to taste

DIRECTIONS

1. Toss potato strips in oil.
2. Add a Crisper pan to the Ninja Foodi.
3. Choose the "Air Fry" function. Set it to 390° F / 200° C for 3 minutes.
4. Press start to preheat.
5. Add potato strips to the Crisper pan.
6. Cook for 25 minutes.
7. Stir and cook for another 20 minutes.

Serving Suggestions:

Serve with ketchup and mayo.

Tips:

Soak potato strips in cold water for 30 minutes before cooking.

Zucchini Strips with Marinara Dip

PREPARATION
20 min

COOKING
30 min

SERVING
8

INGREDIENTS

- 2 zucchinis, sliced into strips
- Salt to taste
- 1 1/2 cups all-purpose flou
- 2 eggs, beaten
- 2 cups bread crumbs
- 2 teaspoons onion powder
- 1 tablespoon garlic powder
- 1/4 cup Parmesan cheese, grated
- 1/2 cup marinara sauce

DIRECTIONS

1. Season zucchini with salt.
2. Let sit for 15 minutes.
3. Pat dry with paper towels.
4. Add flou to a bowl.
5. Add eggs to another bowl.
6. Mix remaining ingredients except for marinara sauce in a third bowl.
7. Dip zucchini strips in the first second, and third bowls.
8. Cover with foil and freeze for 45 minutes.
9. Add Crisper pan inside the Ninja Foodi.
10. Select the "Air Fry" function.
11. Preheat to 360° F / 180° C for 3 minutes.
12. Add zucchini strips to the Crisper pan.
13. Air fry for 20 minutes.
14. Flip and cook for another 10 minutes.
15. Serve with marinara dip.

Serving Suggestions:
Serve with a side salad.

Tips:
Use the reduced-sodium marinara sauce as a dip.

Greek Potatoes

PREPARATION
20 min

COOKING
28 min

SERVING
4

INGREDIENTS

- 1 lb. / 450g potatoes, sliced into wedges
- 2 tablespoons olive oil
- 1 teaspoon paprika
- 2 teaspoons dried oregano
- Salt and pepper to taste
- 1/4 cup onion, diced
- 2 tablespoons lemon juice
- 1 tomato, diced
- 1/4 cup black olives, sliced
- 1/2 cup feta cheese, crumbled

DIRECTIONS

1. Add Crisper pan inside the Ninja Foodi.
2. Choose an "Air Fry" setting.
3. Set it to 390° F / 200° C.
4. Preheat for 3 minutes.
5. While preheating, toss potatoes in oil.
6. Sprinkle it with paprika, oregano, salt, and pepper.
7. Add potatoes to the Crisper pan.
8. Air fry for 18 minutes.
9. Toss and cook for another 5 minutes.
10. Add onion and cook for 5 minutes.
11. Transfer to a bowl.
12. Stir in the rest of the ingredients.

Serving Suggestions:

Garnish with fresh dill.

Tips:

Use freshly squeezed lemon juice.

Garlic Parmesan Fries

PREPARATION
15 min

COOKING
17 min

SERVING
4

INGREDIENTS

- 3 potatoes, sliced into sticks
- 2 tablespoons vegetable oil, divided
- 1/4 cup Parmesan cheese, grated
- 2 cloves garlic, minced
- 1 teaspoon garlic powder
- Salt to taste

DIRECTIONS

1. Coat potato strips with half of the oil.
2. Add Crisper pan inside the Ninja Foodi Grill.
3. Select the "Air Fry" function.
4. Preheat at 360° F / 180° C for 3 minutes.
5. Add fries to the Crisper pan
6. Cook for 12 minutes.
7. Flip and cook for another 5 minutes.
8. Combine the remaining ingredients in a bowl.
9. Toss fries in the mixture and serve.

Serving Suggestions:

Sprinkle with chopped parsley before serving.

Tips:

Use russet potatoes for this recipe.

Fried Garlic Pickles

PREPARATION
20 min

COOKING
15 min

SERVING
6

INGREDIENTS

- 1/4 cup all-purpose flou
- Pinch baking powder
- 2 tablespoons water
- Salt to taste
- 20 dill pickle slices
- 2 tablespoons cornstarch
- 1 1/2 cups panko bread crumbs
- 2 teaspoons garlic powder
- 2 tablespoons canola oil

DIRECTIONS

1. In a bowl, combine flour baking powder, water, and salt.
2. Add more water if the batter is too thick.
3. Put the cornstarch in a second bowl, and mix breadcrumbs and garlic powder in a third bowl.
4. Dip pickles in cornstarch, then in the batter, and finall   dredge with breadcrumb mixture.
5. Add Crisper pan inside the Ninja Foodi.
6. Press "Air Fry" setting.
7. Set it to 360° F / 180° C for 3 minutes.
8. Press "Start" to preheat.
9. Add pickles to the Crisper pan.
10. Brush with oil.
11. Air fry for 10 minutes.
12. Flip, brush with oil, and cook for another 5 minutes.

Serving Suggestions:
Serve with ketchup or sweet chili sauce.

Tips:
Dry pickles before coating with breading.

CHAPTER 14

Staples

Navy Beans with Ham

PREPARATION
5-10 min

COOKING
18 min

SERVING
4

INGREDIENTS

- 1 tablespoon olive oil
- 1 onion, chopped
- 2 carrot, shredded
- 2 tablespoons garlic, minced
- 2 stalks celery, chopped
- 6 cups chicken stock
- 24 oz. / 680g dried navy beans
- 1 teaspoon ground thyme
- 1 teaspoon paprika
- 1 lb. / 450g cooked ham, sliced into small cubes
- 14 oz. / 400g canned diced tomatoes
- Salt and pepper to taste

DIRECTIONS

1. Set the Ninja Foodi to "Sauté". Pour in the oil. Cook the onion and carrot for 2 minutes.
2. Add the garlic and celery. Cook for 3 minutes.
3. Stir in the rest of the ingredients except the ham and tomatoes. Cover the pot.
4. Set it to "Pressure". Cook at "High" pressurc for 10 minutes.
5. Release the pressure naturally. Stir in the tomatoes and ham.
6. Simmer for 5 minutes by pressing the "Sauté" function.

Serving Suggestion:

Serve with crusty bread.

Fried Green Beans

PREPARATION
5 min

COOKING
10 min

SERVING
4

INGREDIENTS

- 1 cup green beans
- 1 tablespoon avocado oil
- 2 tablespoons bread crumbs
- Salt and pepper to taste

DIRECTIONS

1. Toss the green beans in oil. Season with the salt and pepper.
2. Coat with the bread crumbs. "Air Fry" at 390° F / 200° C for 8 minutes.
3. Flip and cook for 2 more minutes.

Serving Suggestion:

Serve as a side dish to the main course.

Baked Beans

PREPARATION
15 min

COOKING
43 min

SERVING
4

INGREDIENTS

- 16 oz. / 450g pinto beans
- 8 cups water
- Salt to taste
- 8 slices bacon
- 1 onion, chopped
- 1/2 red bell pepper, chopped
- 2/3 cup barbecue sauce
- 1/2 cup ketchup
- 2 tablespoons mustard
- 1/4 cup cider vinegar
- 1 teaspoon liquid smoke
- 1/2 cup light brown sugar
- 1/2 cup water

DIRECTIONS

1. Add the beans, 8 cups of water, and salt in the Ninja Foodi. Cover the pot.
2. Set it to "Pressure". Cook at "High" pressure for 25 minutes.
3. Release the pressure naturally. Drain the beans and rinse with cold water.
4. Set the Ninja Foodi to "Sauté". Add the bacon and cook until crispy.
5. Add the bell pepper and onion. Cook for 3 minutes.
6. Add the rest of the ingredients. Cover the pot. Set it to "Pressure". Cook at "High" pressure for 15 minutes. Release the pressure naturally.

Roasted Chickpeas

PREPARATION
10 min

COOKING
21 min

SERVING
4

INGREDIENTS

- 1 can chickpeas, rinsed and drained
- 2 teaspoons olive oil
- 1 teaspoon garlic powder
- 1 teaspoon ground cumin
- 1 teaspoon ground coriander
- 1/8 tsp. ground ginger

DIRECTIONS

1. Coat the beans with oil. Season with all the spices. Place in the Ninja Foodi Cook & Crisp basket.

2. Seal the Crisping lid. Set it to "Air Fry". Cook at 370° F / 190° C for 12 minutes.

3. Stir the chickpeas and cook for another 8 minutes.

4. Stir once more and cook for 1 more minute.

Serving Suggestion:

Mix with other nuts and seeds.

Spicy Green Beans

PREPARATION
4 min

COOKING
12 min

SERVING
4

INGREDIENTS

- 12 oz. / 340g fresh green beans, trimmed
- 1 tablespoon sesame oil
- 1 teaspoon soy sauce
- 1 teaspoon rice wine vinegar
- 1 clove garlic, minced
- 1/2 teaspoon red pepper flake

DIRECTIONS

1. Mix all the ingredients in a large bowl. Marinate for 5 minutes.
2. Place the green beans in the Ninja Foodi Cook & Crisp basket. Seal the crisping lid.
3. Set it to "Air Fry". Cook at 400° F / 205° C for 12 minutes, flippin halfway through.

Serving Suggestion:

Sprinkle toasted garlic chips on top.

Sausage & Beans

PREPARATION
10 min

COOKING
48 min

SERVING
4

INGREDIENTS

- 1 onion, chopped
- 3 stalks celery, chopped
- 1 bay leaf
- 4 carrot, chopped
- 1 sprig fresh rosemary
- 4 sprigs fresh thyme
- 4 cloves garlic, minced
- 1/4 teaspoon oregano, dried
- 1/2 teaspoon pepper
- 6 cups chicken broth
- 1 lb. / 450g white beans
- 1 lb. / 450g chopped sausage roll

DIRECTIONS

1. "Slow Cook" for 3 minutes. Add the rosemary, thyme, garlic, and oregano.
2. Add the sausage and stir-cook to brown evenly.
3. "Slow Cook" for 1 minute. Add the pepper and stir in broth. "Slow Cook" for 5 minutes.
4. Stir in the white beans. Lock the lid in place.
5. Set it to "Pressure".
6. Cook at "High" pressure for 40 minutes. Release the pressure naturally.

Tomato & Beans

PREPARATION
12 min

COOKING
42 min

SERVING
4

INGREDIENTS

- 4 slices bacon, chopped
- 1 onion, chopped
- 2 cloves garlic, minced
- 1 bay leaf
- Salt to taste
- 2 1/4 cups dry cannellini beans
- 28 oz. / 800g tomatoes
- 6 oz. / 170g tomato paste
- 2 cups chicken broth

DIRECTIONS

1. Set the Ninja Foodi to "Sauté". Cook the bacon until crispy. Add the onion and garlic.

2. Cook for 2 minutes. Add the rest of the ingredients. Cover the pot. Set it to "Pressure".

3. Cook at "High" pressure for 40 minutes. Release the pressure naturally.

4. Season with salt and pepper.

Serving Suggestion:

Top with the feta cheese.

Lemon Butter Green Beans

PREPARATION
7 min

COOKING
10 min

SERVING
4

INGREDIENTS

- 1 lb. / 450g green beans
- 2 tablespoons olive oil
- 2 cloves garlic
- 1/4 cup lemon
- 1 tablespoon Parmesan cheese
- 2 tablespoons butter
- Salt and pepper to taste

DIRECTIONS

1. Place the beans in a bowl. Coat with the oil. Season with the salt and pepper.

2. Put the green beans in the Ninja Foodi Cook & Crisp basket.

3. Cook at 390° F / 200° C for 10 minutes, flippin halfway through.

4. Make the sauce by simmering the rest of the ingredients in the pot by pressing "Sauté" for 3 to 5 minutes.

Sensational Carrot Puree

PREPARATION
10 min

COOKING
4 min

SERVING
4

INGREDIENTS

- 1 1/2 lb. / 680g carrots, chopped
- 1 tablespoon of butter at room temperature
- 1 tablespoon of agave nectar
- 1/4 teaspoon of sea salt
- 1 cup of water

DIRECTIONS

1. Clean and peel your carrots properly. Roughly chop up them into small pieces

2. Add 1 cup of water to your Removable Cooking Pot

3. Place the carrots in Ninja Foodi Removable Cooking Pot and place into the Ninja Foodi

4. Lock up the lid and cook on "High" pressure for 4 minutes. Perform a quick release

5. Transfer the carrots to a deep bowl and use an immersion blender to blend the carrots

6. Add butter, nectar, salt, and puree. Taste the puree and season more if needed. Enjoy!

Simple Broccoli Florets

PREPARATION
10 min

COOKING
6 min

SERVING
4

INGREDIENTS

- 4 tablespoons butter, melted
- Salt and pepper to taste
- 2 lb. / 900g broccoli floret
- 1 cup whipping cream

DIRECTIONS

1. Place a steamer basket in your Ninja Foodi (bottom part) and add water
2. Place florets on top of the basket and lock the lid
3. Cook on "High" pressure for 6 minutes. Quick-release pressure
4. Transfer florets from the steamer basket to the pot. Add salt, pepper, butter, and stir
5. Lock crisping lid and cook on "Air Fry" mode for 360° F / 180° C. Serve and enjoy!

CHAPTER 15

Desserts

Strawberry Crumble

PREPARATION
15 min

COOKING
120 min

SERVING
5

INGREDIENTS

- 1 cup almond flou
- 2 tablespoons butter, melted
- 8-10 drops liquid stevia
- 3-4 cups fresh strawberries, hulled and sliced
- 1 tablespoon butter, chopped

DIRECTIONS

1. Lightly, grease the pot of Ninja Foodi.
2. In a bowl, add the flour melted butter, and stevia and mix until a crumbly mixture forms.
3. In the pot of the prepared Ninja Foodi, place the strawberry slices and dot with chopped butter.
4. Spread the flou mixture on top evenly
5. Close the Ninja Foodi with the crisping lid and select "Slow Cooker".
6. Set on "Low" for 2 hours.
7. Press "Start/Stop" to begin cooking.
8. Place the pan onto a wire rack to cool slightly.

Lovely Rum Sundae

PREPARATION
10 min

COOKING
8 min

SERVING
4

INGREDIENTS

- Vanilla ice cream for serving
- 1 pineapple, cored and sliced
- 1 teaspoon cinnamon, ground
- ½ cup brown sugar, packed
- ½ cup dark rum

DIRECTIONS

1. Take a large deep bowl and add sugar, cinnamon, and rum
2. Add the pineapple in the layer, dredge them properly, and make sure that they are coated well
3. Preheat your Foodi in "Grill" mode at "Max", setting the timer to 8 minutes
4. Once you hear the beep, strain any additional rum from the pineapple slices and transfer them to the grill rate of your appliance
5. Press them down and grill for 8 minutes. Make sure to not overcrowd the grill grate, cook in batches if needed
6. Top each of the ring with a scoop of your favorite ice cream, sprinkle a bit of cinnamon on top
7. Enjoy!

Grilled Donuts

PREPARATION
15 min

COOKING
8 min

SERVING
8

INGREDIENTS

- 1/4 cup milk
- 1 teaspoon vanilla extract
- 2 cups powdered sugar
- 16 oz. / 450g prepared biscuit dough
- Cooking spray

DIRECTIONS

1. In a bowl, mix milk, vanilla, and sugar.
2. Cut rings from the prepared dough.
3. Refrigerate for 5 minutes.
4. Add grill grate to the Ninja Foodi.
5. Choose a "Grill" setting.
6. Set it to "Med"
7. Preheat for 6 minutes.
8. Spray round dough with oil.
9. Add to the grill and cook for 4 minutes.
10. Dip in the milk mixture and grill for another 4 minutes.

Serving Suggestions:

Sprinkle with cinnamon sugar or chocolate sprinkles before serving.

275

Cashew Cream

PREPARATION
18 min

COOKING
10 min

SERVING
10

INGREDIENTS

- 3 cups cashew
- 2 cups chicken stock
- 1 teaspoon salt
- 1 tablespoon butter
- 2 tablespoons ricotta cheese

DIRECTIONS

1. Combine the cashews with the chicken stock in the Multicooker.

2. Add salt and close the Ninja Foodi lid. Cook the dish on the "Pressure" mode for 10 minutes.

3. Remove the cashews from the Multicooker and drain the nuts from the water. Transfer the cashews to a blender and add the ricotta cheese and butter.

4. Blend the mixture until it is smooth. When you get the texture you want, remove it from a blender. Serve it immediately or keep the cashew butter in the refrigerator.

A Fruit Salad to Die For

PREPARATION
5-10 min

COOKING
4 min

SERVING
4

INGREDIENTS

- 2 peaches, pitted and sliced
- 1 can (9 oz. / 255g) pineapple chunks, drained, juice reserved
- ½ lb. / 225g strawberries washed, hulled, and halved
- 1 tablespoon freshly squeezed lime juice
- 6 tablespoons honey, divided

DIRECTIONS

1. Add pineapple, peaches, strawberries, and ½ of honey, toss well
2. Preheat your Ninja Foodi by pressing the "Grill" option and setting it to "Max"
3. Set the timer to 4 minutes
4. Allow it to preheat until it beeps
5. Transfer fruits to Grill grate and close the lid
6. Cook for 4 minutes
7. Add remaining 3 tablespoons of honey, lime juice, 1 tablespoon reserved pineapple juice into a small-sized bowl
8. Once cooked, place fruits in a large-sized bowl and toss with honey mixture
9. Serve and enjoy!

Cinnamon Bun

PREPARATION
25 min

COOKING
15 min

SERVING
8

INGREDIENTS

- 1 cup almond flou
- ½ teaspoon baking powder
- 3 tablespoon Erythritol
- 2 tablespoon ground cinnamon
- ½ teaspoon vanilla extract
- 1 tablespoon butter
- 1 egg, whisked
- ¾ teaspoon salt
- ¼ cup almond milk

DIRECTIONS

1. Mix up together the almond flour baking powder, vanilla extract, egg, salt, and almond milk.
2. Knead the soft and non-sticky dough.
3. Roll up the dough with the help of the rolling pin
4. Sprinkle dough with the butter, cinnamon, and Erythritol.
5. Roll the dough into the log.
6. Cut the roll into 7 pieces.
7. Spray multi-cooker basket with cooking spray.
8. Place the cinnamon buns in the basket and close the lid.
9. Set the "Bake" mode and cook the buns for 15 minutes at 360° F / 180° C
10. Check if the buns are cooked with the help of the toothpick.
11. Chill the buns well and serve!

Strawberry & Cake Kebabs

PREPARATION
15 min

COOKING
6 min

SERVING
5

INGREDIENTS

- 1 pack white cake mix
- 2 cups strawberries, sliced in half
- 2 tablespoons honey
- 1/4 cup sugar
- Cooking spray

DIRECTIONS

1. Cook cake mix according to the directions in the box.
2. Insert the grill grate in the Ninja Foodi.
3. Choose a "Grill" setting.
4. Preheat at 325° F / 160° C for 15 minutes.
5. While waiting, slice the cake into cubes.
6. Toss strawberries in honey and sugar.
7. Thread cake cubes and strawberries alternately onto skewers.
8. Grill for 3 minutes per side.

Serving Suggestions:

Serve with vanilla ice cream.

Tips:

When preparing the cake mix, you can replace water with pudding to make the cake thicker.

Cinnamon Donuts

PREPARATION
15 min

COOKING
6 min

SERVING
8

INGREDIENTS

- ½ cup granulated sugar
- 1 tablespoon ground cinnamon
- 1 (16 oz. / 450g) can flak   large biscuits
- Olive oil cooking spray
- 4 tablespoons unsalted butter, melted

DIRECTIONS

1. Line a baking sheet with parchment paper.
2. In a shallow dish, mix the sugar and cinnamon. Set aside.
3. Remove the biscuits from the can and carefully separate them.
4. Place 4 donuts onto the lightly greased cooking pan in a single layer.
5. Arrange the Crisper pan at the bottom of the Ninja Foodi.
6. Select "Air Fry" and then adjust the temperature to 350° F / 175° C.
7. Set the timer for 6 minutes and press the "Start"
8. When the display shows "Add Food" insert the cooking tray in the center position.
9. When the display shows "Turn Food," turn the donuts.
10. When cooking time is complete, remove the tray from the Ninja Foodi.
11. Brush both sides of the warm donuts with melted butter and then coat with cinnamon sugar.
12. Repeat with the remaining donuts.
13. Serve warm.

Chocolate Brownies

PREPARATION
15 min

COOKING
15 min

SERVING
4

INGREDIENTS

- ½ cup all-purpose flou
- ¾ cup sugar
- 6 tablespoons unsweetened cocoa powder
- ¼ teaspoon baking powder
- ¼ teaspoon salt
- ¼ cup unsalted butter, melted
- 2 large eggs
- 1 tablespoon vegetable oil
- ½ teaspoon vanilla extract

DIRECTIONS

1. Grease a 7 inch / 18 cm baking pan generously. Set aside.
2. In a bowl, add all the ingredients and mix until well combined.
3. Place the mixture into the prepared baking pan, and with the back of a spoon, smooth the top surface.
4. Arrange the Crisper pan at the bottom of the Ninja Foodi.
5. Select "Air Fry" and then adjust the temperature to 330° F / 165° C.
6. Set the timer for 15 minutes and press the "Start"
7. When the display shows "Add Food" place the baking pan over the Crisper pan.
8. When the display shows "Turn Food" do nothing.
9. When cooking time is complete, remove the pan from the Ninja Foodi and place onto a wire rack to cool completely before cutting.
10. Cut the brownie into desired-sized squares and serve.

Grilled Apple Pie

PREPARATION
30 min

COOKING
28 min

SERVING
8

INGREDIENTS

- 8 cups cold water
- 1 tablespoon lemon juice
- 8 apples, diced
- 1/2 cup brown sugar
- 1/2 teaspoon ground cinnamon
- 1/2 teaspoon ground ginger
- 3 tablespoons all-purpose flou
- 1/2 cup applesauce
- 1 frozen pie crust

DIRECTIONS

1. In a bowl, mix water, lemon juice, and apples.
2. Let sit for 10 minutes.
3. Drain and pat dry.
4. Add Grill grate to Ninja Foodi.
5. Press "Grill" setting.
6. Set it to the "Max" and preheat for 8 minutes.
7. Coat apples with sugar.
8. Grill for 8 minutes without flipping
9. In a bowl, combine the remaining ingredients.
10. Stir in grilled apples.
11. Pour the mixture into a small baking pan.
12. Top with the pie crust.
13. Select the "Bake" setting.
14. Cook pie at 350° F / 175° C for 20 minutes.

Serving Suggestions:

Serve with vanilla ice cream.

Tips:

Defrost pie crust before using.

Marshmallow Banana Boat

PREPARATION
19 min

COOKING
6 min

SERVING
4

INGREDIENTS

- ½ cup peanut butter chips
- 1/3 cup chocolate chips
- 1 cup mini marshmallow
- 4 ripe bananas

DIRECTIONS

1. Take the banana and slice them gently, keeping the peel
2. Make sure to not cut it all the way through
3. Use your hands to carefully peel the banana skin like a book, revealing the banana flesh
4. Divide your marshmallow, peanut butter, chocolate chips among the prepared bananas, stuff them well
5. Preheat in "Grill" mode at "Med", and set the timer to 6 minutes
6. Once you hear a beep, transfer your prepared bananas to the Grill grate, cook for 6 minutes until the chocolate melts well
7. Serve and enjoy!

Blackberry Cake

PREPARATION
35 min

COOKING
20 min

SERVING
4

INGREDIENTS

- 4 tablespoons butter
- 3 tablespoon Erythritol
- 1 oz. / 28g blackberries
- 1 cup almond flou
- ½ teaspoon baking powder

DIRECTIONS

1. Combine all the liquid ingredients.
2. Then add baking powder, almond flour and Erythritol.
3. Stir the mixture until smooth.
4. Add blackberries and stir the batter gently with the help of the spoon.
5. Take the non-stick springform pan and transfer the batter inside.
6. Place the baking pan in the pot and lower the Crisping lid.
7. "Bake" the cake for 20 minutes at 365° F / 185°C.
8. Chill it little and serve!

The Original Pot-De-Crème

PREPARATION
30 min

COOKING
12 min

SERVING
4

INGREDIENTS

- 6 egg yolks
- 2 cups heavy whip cream
- 1/3 cup cocoa powder
- 1 tablespoon pure vanilla extract
- ½ teaspoon liquid stevia
- Whipped coconut cream as needed for garnish
- Shaved dark chocolate, for garnish

DIRECTIONS

1. Take a medium bowl and whisk in yolks, heavy cream, cocoa powder, vanilla, and stevia

2. Pour the mixture into the Loaf Pan and place it inside Ninja Foodi

3. Add enough water to reach about halfway up the sides of the Loaf Pan

4. Lock lid and cook on "High" pressure for 12 minutes

5. Quick-release pressure once the cycle is complete

6. Remove the Loaf Pan from the insert and let it cool

7. Chill the dessert in the refrigerator and serve with a garnish of whipped coconut cream and shaved dark chocolate

8. Enjoy!

Stuffed Baked Apples

PREPARATION
3 min

COOKING
12 min

SERVING
4

INGREDIENTS

- 4 tbsps. honey
- ¼ c. brown sugar
- ½ c. raisins
- ½ c. crushed walnuts
- 4 large apples

DIRECTIONS

1. Preheat in "Air Fry" mode at 350°F / 175°C.
2. Cut the apples from the stem and remove the inner using a spoon.
3. Now fil each apple with raisins, walnuts, honey, and brown sugar.
4. Transfer apples in a pan and place in an Cook & Crisp basket, cook for 12 minutes.
5. Serve.

Peanut Butter Cups

PREPARATION
5 min

COOKING
3 min

SERVING
4

INGREDIENTS

- 4 graham crackers
- 4 peanut butter cups
- 4 marshmallows

DIRECTIONS

1. Add a Crisper pan to Ninja Foodi.
2. Choose the "Air Fry" function.
3. Preheat at 360° F / 180° C for 3 minutes.
4. Break the crackers in half.
5. Add crackers to the Crisper pan.
6. Top with the peanut butter cups.
7. Cook for 2 minutes.
8. Sprinkle marshmallows on top and cook for another 1 minute.
9. Top with the remaining crackers and serve.

Serving Suggestions:

Serve with warm milk.

Tips:

You can also use chocolate spread in place of peanut butter cups if you like.

Original French Pineapple Toast

PREPARATION
5-10 min

COOKING
16 min

SERVING
4

INGREDIENTS

- 10 bread slices
- ¼ cup of sugar
- ¼ cup milk
- 3 large whole eggs
- 1 cup of coconut milk
- 10 slices pineapple, peeled
- ½ cup coconut flake
- Cooking spray as needed

DIRECTIONS

1. Take a mixing bowl and whisk in coconut milk, sugar, eggs, milk and stir well
2. Dup breads in the mixture and keep the mon the side for 2 minutes
3. Preheat Ninja Foodi selecting "Grill" at "Med" and set timer to 16 minutes
4. Let it preheat until you hear a beep
5. Arrange bread slices over the grill grate, lock lid, and cook for 2 minutes. Flip and cook for 2 minutes more
6. Repeat with remaining slices, serve, and enjoy!

CONCLUSION

This cookbook has offered you a large array of recipes using a new cooking appliance; the revolutionary Ninja Foodi, which combines pressure cookers, Air Fryers, Ovens, and Dehydrator at the same time.

As you can see, the Ninja Foodi is a versatile and multi-functional cooking device that lets you cook food in various ways. The Ninja Foodi will let you savor delectable grilled steaks and burgers inside the comfort of your home anytime. That's not all. It also helps ensure that you create only the healthiest and delicious dishes for yourself and your family.

With this device, you can get started on a healthier lifestyle without putting too much burden and stress on yourself. You can whip up healthy dishes without having to spend too much time inside the kitchen.

With virtually no smoke, all your favorite dishes may be grilled, roasted, and air fried. The Ninja Foodi is made of polished stainless steel and has a domed lid of black plastic.

If you liked this recipes cookbook please leave a review!
Many thanks to chef Brian Warren for his precious advices.

Made in the USA
Middletown, DE
03 November 2022